NO LIMIT

NO LIMIT

The Texas Hold 'Em Guide
to Winning in Business

DONALD G. KRAUSE

AND

JEFF CARTER

AMACOM AMERICAN MANAGEMENT ASSOCIATION
New York ♦ Atlanta ♦ Brussels ♦ Chicago ♦ Mexico City ♦ San Francisco
Shanghai ♦ Tokyo ♦ Toronto ♦ Washington, D. C.

This publication is designed to provide accurate and authoritative information in regard to the subject matter covered. It is sold with the understanding that the publisher is not engaged in rendering legal, accounting, or other professional service. If legal advice or other expert assistance is required, the services of a competent professional person should be sought.

Library of Congress Cataloging-in-Publication Data

Krause, Donald G.
  No limit : the Texas hold 'em guide to winning in business / Donald G. Krause and Jeff Carter.
    p. cm.
Includes index.
ISBN-13: 978-0-8144-8064-9
ISBN-10: 0-8144-8064-0
  1. Strategic planning. 2. Management. 3. Success in business. I. Title.

HD30.28.K7219 2008
658.4'09—dc22

2007045867

Printing number
10 9 8 7 6 5 4 3 2 1

For my beautiful wife, Myndi, and son Sam, the inspiration that keeps me dreaming.

And a special thank you to Jeff Miller for pushing me to attempt this endeavor.

—Jeff Carter

In memory of Evelyn Elizabeth Bradshaw and Elizabeth Lorraine Krause. And for my wonderful wife of 15 years, Susan Ruth Bradshaw, who grows more lovely with each passing day.

—Don Krause

CONTENTS

1 Why Use the Poker Paradigm 1

2 Poker 101: The Concepts of Texas
Hold 'em Strategy 16

PART ONE: POSITION . . . . **.27**

3 Building Confidence 29

4 Anger, Frustration, and Fear 37

5 The Role of Luck 45

6 Using Logic to Make Good Decisions 56

7 Avoiding Errors 65

8 Requirements, Risk, and Reward 75

PART TWO: OPPORTUNITY **85**

9 The Land of OZ: Classifying Players 87

10 Getting to Know You 96

11 Pre-Flop Concepts 106

PART THREE: KINETICS **117**

12 Evaluating the Flop: I. Reading Pocket Cards. 119

13 Evaluating the Flop: II. Reading the Board,
Counting Outs, and Computing Pot Odds 128

14 Evaluating the Flop: III. Playing Decisions 137

15 The SWORD in Hand: Tactics I 148

16 The SWORD in Hand: Tactics II 159

17 The SWORD in Hand: Tactics III 169

PART FOUR: END GAME AND RESULTS. **177**

18 Drowning in the River 179

19 Dimensions of Bluffing: I. Bluffing in Hold 'Em 186

20 Dimensions of Bluffing:
II. Bluffing in Interpersonal Competition 193

21 Survival of the Fittest 206

Appendix A: Texas Hold 'Em Fundamentals 213

Appendix B: Pocket Scores 216

Appendix C: The Thirty-Six Stratagems 219

Index 223

NO LIMIT

♠ ♣ ♡ ◇

1

Why Use the Poker Paradigm?

Whether he likes it or not, a man's character is stripped bare at the poker table; if the other players read him better than he does, he has only himself to blame. Unless he is both able and prepared to see himself as others do, flaws and all, he will be a loser in cards, as in life.

—Anthony Holden, *Big Deal*

THE GAME of poker is tightly woven into the fabric of American culture and history. Can you understand the following sentence? "That guy may have upped the ante, but I have an ace in the hole, and will call his bluff when the chips are down!" Of course you can! Phrases like "ace in the hole," "calling a bluff," "when the chips are down," and "up the ante" all originate from poker. Each year, thousands of people visit Deadwood, South Dakota, a fairly out-of-the-way place, to see the table where Wild Bill Hickok was shot in the back while holding the infamous "dead man's hand" (that is, two pair: aces and eights). Many popular TV programs and movies have a poker theme: the old western series, *Maverick* (and the more recent

feature movie of the same title); *The Gambler* TV movie series; *Tilt;*
Deadwood; and *Rounders;* to name a few.

With the advent of television coverage of big money poker tournaments, Texas Hold 'em poker is now the most popular and well-
known variety of the game in the world. Millions of people play
Texas Hold 'em every day on the Internet. Millions more are interested in learning the game.

What are the characteristics of Texas Hold 'em that make the game
a suitable foundation for learning strategies and tactics that can be
used to win in situations involving critical business, career, wealth,
power, and relationship issues? Texas Hold 'em is a game that com-
bines a large variety of challenging factors in a particularly fascinating
way. At some point during almost every Texas Hold 'em session, a
player will be required to confront the best and worst in himself and
in others: grit and greed, discipline and deception, fact and fancy,
hope and hate, angst and ecstasy. At the same time, he must juggle
calculation of complex odds and deal with the occasional (okay,
maybe more than occasional) oddball personality at the table.

Mastering the skills required to triumph in the intensely and personally competitive environment found at the poker table requires
both study and practice, but the rewards in terms of self-satisfaction
(not to mention extra dollars) are worth the effort. More important,
the skills and strategies that bring success at Texas Hold 'em are
exactly those skills and strategies which will bring success in competitive situations from business, career, wealth, power, and relationship
areas of life. (Within the context of this book, we will refer to competitive situations in business, career, wealth, power, and relationships as "interpersonal competition." Much of what we say, however,
can be readily applied to interorganizational competition as well.)

The conditions, challenges, and decisions faced during a session
of Hold 'em are a structured microcosm of the conditions, challenges, and decisions faced time and again in every career, every
business, and every relationship when we are competing with others.
The psychology and science practiced by a winning Hold 'em player
is identical to the psychology and science practiced by every successful competitive person.

By using Texas Hold 'em poker as a model, we can immediately grasp a clear structure for conveying ideas about competitive strategy and tactics, in the context of an internationally popular and readily understood game played for significant and real stakes. The problem with teaching competitive concepts when examples depend on historical studies of war or business is that the situations used as a basis for explanation have not been, nor ever will be, encountered by most readers. With Hold 'em as a teaching vehicle, examples and situations used for purposes of illustration have already been, or eventually will be, experienced by most readers in the course of playing the game.

Practice precedes mastery. If you are willing to practice long enough to master even a few of the ideas we present here, you will be pleasantly surprised at how much better you play the game of interpersonal competition.

Making Decisions in Competitive Situations

Decisions are the basic human activities that drive results toward, or away from, objectives. The outcomes of decisions about investing one's time, influence, and assets inevitably increase or decrease personal wealth and power. Further, each and every money and power decision, regardless of the specifics of the situation, is made within the context of competition.

In every aspect of life where power and wealth are at stake, there is always competition, though in many cases participants in commonplace exchanges may not need to acknowledge that fact. To succeed in gaining and holding wealth and power, however, you must develop and maintain an acute sensitivity to the competitive aspects of the wealth and power transactions that are constantly happening around you and how you are affected by them. The decisions you make in these competitive transactions, even if seemingly trivial, determine how well and quickly you advance toward your goals.

The social and economic transactions that occur constantly among people, whether simple and commonplace or complex and unusual, are, in effect, negotiations from which an exchange of wealth, power, and service occurs. Prevailing societal norms and traditions often predetermine the outcome of everyday negotiations, but that does not mean these negotiation opportunities should be ignored. Common sense dictates that the more often you are able to channel a transaction in a direction that is advantageous to you, the stronger your wealth, power, and relationship attributes become.

In his book, *The Theory of Poker*, poker philosopher David Sklansky introduced a concept he called the "Fundamental Theorem of Poker." The theorem states:

> Every time you play a hand *differently* from the way you would have played it if you could see all your opponents' cards, they (your opponents) gain; and every time you play a hand *the same* way you would have played it if you could see all their cards, they (your opponents) lose. Conversely, every time opponents play their hands *differently* from the way they would have if they could see all your cards, you gain; and every time they play their hands *the same* way they would have played if they could see all your cards, you lose.

This brings us to the point of *No Limit*. Sklansky's "Fundamental Theorem of Poker" suggests the following "General Theorem of Interpersonal Competition," whose four parts might be stated like this:

Part 1:
Every time you complete a move that convinces, compels, induces, or motivates another person to act in a way that benefits you, *when he would not have acted otherwise,* you gain.

Part 2:
Every time you fail to complete a move that convinces, compels, induces, or motivates another person to act in a way that benefits you, *when the move could and should have been made,* you lose.

Part 3:
Every time another person completes a move that is not to your benefit, *when you could and should have blocked the move,* you lose.

Part 4:
Every time you are able to prevent another person from completing a move that is not to your benefit, *when you could and should have blocked the move,* you gain.

No Limit is a handbook for effectively implementing this "General Theorem of Interpersonal Competition." Over the course of the next 200 or so pages, we—the authors—will build a model, or paradigm, for quickly developing and executing effective decisions under a wide variety of competitive situations, using Texas Hold 'em poker as a canvas for understanding concepts and applications. The resulting paradigm will incorporate the most effective strategic and tactical principles from masters of strategy and tactics like Sun Tzu, Clausewitz, Musashi, Machiavelli, T. E. Lawrence, Mao Tse-tung, Tom Peters, and Peter Drucker, not to mention many modern-day poker theorists (like David Sklansky above). You can use this paradigm every day to improve your odds for success in your business, in your career, and in your relationships.

If you can understand how to play and win at Hold 'em, you can understand how to play and win at the business of life, the business of wealth, and the business of power. If you apply our suggested strategies in the competitive arenas of life, that is, if you are willing to approach wealth, power, and relationship decisions using the Poker Paradigm developed in *No Limit,* you will find yourself holding stronger hands, from better positions, on a more consistent basis, and therefore winning more pots than your opponents.

Because the game of Hold 'em itself fosters disciplined thinking under conditions of uncertainty and competition, when you finish this book you will hold a distinct advantage over competitors—especially over those who do not have a structured and effective approach to evaluating strategy and tactics for competitive decision making. The material contained in *No Limit* will make it easy for you to apply winning Hold 'em tactics to any competitive situation or decision you may face, whether in the card room, the boardroom, or your living room.

Simplifying Assumptions

Building a decision model requires you to condense reality into a relative handful of carefully defined correlations using a small number of simplifying assumptions to filter out unwanted (and hopefully irrelevant) chaos. The simplifying assumptions, then, govern the results and conclusions produced by the model and, thereby, limit possible outcomes to those allowed within the definitions of reality created by those assumptions. To the extent that the simplifying assumptions do not, in fact, represent reality, the model will produce inaccurate and probably useless results.

At least two important views about the nature of reality underlie the results and conclusions of the model we are presenting here.

First view: Rewards for winning in the world of wealth, power, and relationship issues are similar to and can be measured much like winning in the world of Texas Hold 'em. Further, individuals reading *No Limit* are interested in those rewards. We feel the first view is true for situations we intend to include within the scope of this book. Wealth and status, for instance, tend to follow success in poker, business, career, or relationships, while other rewards, like going to heaven (which is not covered in the scope of the book) may or may not follow success in worldly endeavors. We assume that in reading this book, you are seeking tangible, mundane wealth and prestige in addition to whatever other objectives you may have.

Second view: The principles for winning at Texas Hold 'em poker can be transferred effectively to the world of wealth, power, and relationship issues. Obviously, poker is a card game for people to play. The game includes a fixed set of rules designed to set up a winner and a loser through structured competition. Businesses, careers, and relationships are not playgrounds, nor are they games. They do not have easily understood or fixed rules. But wealth, power, and relationship decision situations, like those in poker, produce competition among people resulting in winners and losers. As a consequence, competitive skills for winning at poker and competitive skills for winning in the world of interpersonal conflict are remarkably similar. For example, the ability to bluff is an absolutely essential ability for winning in every competitive arena. We will detail many aspects of bluffing in later chapters.

We assume, then, that the poker world and the wealth, power, relationship world are connected tightly enough to make a transfer of skills highly rewarding. Persons who understand how to apply winning tactics from the poker table to business, career, and relationship issues and back again will succeed more often than those who do not. This book will specifically provide you with that understanding.

Using Keywords

Two critical elements of an effective paradigm, or model, are clarity and usability. In the pages that follow, we will cover hundreds of concepts that are related in one way or another to the overall goal of helping you achieve better results in competitive situations. In an effort to improve clarity and usability, given the large number of ideas covered, we have adopted the convention of creating keywords to serve as mnemonics for conveniently associating major groups of concepts.

The keywords presented here are designed to help you remember the concepts covered, not to be cute or entertaining (well, maybe a little entertaining). Our objective is to provide you with a compact, coherent, and easy-to-remember set of tools, which you can use, particularly in stressful competitive situations, to maintain a steady focus and keep yourself on track—whether you are playing $10/$20 No Limit Hold 'em at the Bellagio or working through a deal on Wall Street involving your life's savings or long-term career prospects.

Organization of the Book

The central and overarching keyword is the word P-O-K-E-R.

··
The principles represented within the key word P-O-K-E-R are:

Position
Opportunity

Kinetics (the study of motion or activity)

End Game

Results

....

The book will be set up in four Parts based on the five P-O-K-E-R principles.

PART ONE: POSITION

This section focuses on critical aspects of character and attitude and how these aspects affect your ability to win at Hold 'em and at business. Character and attitude are essential building blocks of achievement; they are part of the stake you bring to the table. *Character* and *attitude* have already been established by the time you sit down to play. The intensity of competition and the multifaceted dynamics involved in winning against smart, talented opponents demand insight into developing and managing character, both your opponents' and your own.

Character, in the context we are using the word, has nothing to do with ethics or morality. The cards have no creed. And it is the same with the character of success. Character here refers only to that set of personal attributes that can contribute to, or detract from, higher levels of competitive performance. Many people treat character as if it were an accident of nature. This is emphatically not true! Your character is your fault, your responsibility, and your choice.

Further, while we strongly advocate selecting and nurturing self-defined aspects of character, we are absolutely not recommending that you adopt any particular set of attributes, nor are we suggesting that there is an ideal or perfect set available. Instead, we recommend that you select those features, or attributes, of character that you feel will enhance your own performance the most. We may emphasize approaches that seem (to us) to work better than others under certain conditions. But you must investigate for yourself and choose for yourself.

The distance you travel along the road to success in Hold 'em, and in everything else too, is largely determined by the depth of your commitment to a set of carefully selected character attributes that lend themselves to greater accomplishment within the context of the game you play, the people you play with, and the level of stakes you intend to risk.

If you were to consider life an automobile road trip, character would be the type of car you drive, while attitude would be the process you use to navigate and steer. Are you careful? Careless? Do you plan ahead, or just wing it? Do you think the other drivers are jerks whom you must somehow defeat to get where you are going, or are you inclined to civility and courtesy? Attitude describes the methods and approaches you apply in response to the stop signs, speed limits, expressways, crossroads, and detours you will inevitably face on your trip to success. Attitude defines how you react to others and how others react to you. Attitude in itself may not define success, but it certainly defines the route you will take in getting there.

PART TWO: OPPORTUNITY

A wise Oriental philosopher once said, "Opportunity emerges when the winds of chance blow the dust of good fortune in our direction." He failed to note, however, that we are more than likely blinded by all that gusting wind and billowing dirt. As a result, whatever kind of opportunity is hiding within that particular cloud of dust sails right on by, unseen and unappreciated.

The material included in the Opportunity section will help you cut through the grit and grime of everyday challenges and identify the beginnings of situations that are favorable to increased success. From a Hold 'em perspective, we will deal with a number of the many aspects of opening-hand selection and betting before the flop. From a wealth and power perspective, we will cover how opportunity comes into focus, indicators of real opportunity, and warning signs for pitfalls, scams, and guaranteed failures.

The Opportunity section focuses on developing a basic strategy for approaching pre-flop Hold 'em which can then be transferred to everyday situations. When appropriately combined, the topics of the first two sections—position and opportunity—provide the vision required to set objectives and chart a strategy toward a specified result over a period of time. Success in particular instances may be considered the result of chance or good luck; however, chance or good luck is usually supported by a strong base of conscientious effort. The person who works most effectively toward developing himself in his areas of interest tends to be the luckiest in the long run.

Again, definite choices of strategic method are yours. After all, it's your money and your life at stake. However, beyond the basic principles of winning play (which we cover in Chapter 2, Poker 101), there are a wide variety of alternative strategies available—enough to accommodate any life objective and any personal style.

For instance, in wealth and power situations and in Hold 'em, you can choose to be a generally tight player who plays mostly premium pocket-card combinations, or you can choose to be a generally loose player, with the exact calibration of your style depending upon table limits and individuals involved. It is probably not a good idea to play loose or tight indiscriminately or randomly because the attitude associated with winning for each of these styles is different. (The exception is when you play with the same group of people repeatedly, which is more common in life and career circumstances than in the casino. Unmanaged predictability is deadly for poker players and equally dangerous where wealth and power are at stake. Tactical predictability, or more accurately, *unpredictability*, however, is the cornerstone of successful high-stakes bluffing.)

PART THREE: KINETICS

Kinetics is defined as the relationships of power between the people in a group and the forces that tend to produce activity and change in a situation. We titled the third part of the P-O-K-E-R keyword "Kinetics" because it covers how the dynamics of interaction mold and direct the nature and evolution of the competition.

With respect to Hold 'em, we discuss the kinetics of the flop and the first post-flop betting round. Everything changes when the flop cards are revealed. Good hands often become trash and trash often becomes golden. The flop is a force of change. Your ability to understand the magnitude and direction of that force will determine your ultimate success in the game. Next to selecting effective (for you) opening card combinations, correctly evaluating the flop in relation to your own hand and reasonably assessing the consequences of the flop for others' hands are the most important elements of playing the game.

For wealth and power situations, the dynamics of the flop is similar to the dynamics surrounding the initial rounds in a negotiation or competition, when the relative strength of parties involved begins to be revealed. Perceptions of strength are based on the actions and communications of parties involved.

Unlike Hold 'em, where each player has the same chance of success before the pocket cards are dealt, real life situations rarely involve competitions in which players have equal strength. A good deal of the time you will enter into a competitive situation in the belief that your position is fairly strong, only to find out that other parties were hiding their true strength or that you have made several less-than-accurate assumptions.

As you are able to perceive additional or different aspects of relative strength, your strategy and tactics may require alteration and evolution. Your ability to attack or defend may be enhanced or weakened. Understanding the forces at work within the context of the conditions that exist, or at least appear to exist, is critical to directing assets to most effective use.

The Kinetics section describes tactics needed to win at Hold 'em and in business, career, wealth, power, and relationship contests. Tactics are short-term actions and reactions which are undertaken in response to specific situations in order to attain longer-term objectives. Your overall strategy is the context or fabric which encompasses your tactical maneuvers. As Sun Tzu noted 2500 years ago, tactics and strategy flow one from the other in a continuous stream. They cannot be easily separated.

You must realize and understand immediately that for every tactic under the sun, there is a countertactic that will defeat it. No tactic works every time. The *second truth* of competitive situations is (the first truth is revealed later in the text) when your opponent knows what you are doing, and no matter how powerful your position, he can threaten it, or perhaps even defeat it. The *third truth* of competitive situations is that you cannot trust anything your opponent tells or shows you. The *fourth truth* of competitive situations is that your opponent is neither as smart nor as stupid as he appears to be. And the *fifth truth* is that neither are you.

The critical point is that successful application of tactics is based on objectivity and humility (that's right, humility!). Humility and objectivity go hand in hand. Objectivity, particularly in high-pressure situations, requires evenness of temperament and emotional control. The practice of humility is the most reliable way to achieve evenness of temperament and emotional control. The practice of humility does not mean you allow others to run over you. Rather, it means bowing to the requirements of reality. Sometimes in business you must back down to get ahead. Sometimes in Hold 'em you have to fold pocket kings because you are clearly beaten. If you cannot do what you must do when the time comes, you cannot expect to win over the long run.

True humility allows a person to evaluate and manage himself objectively, especially when it is necessary to take a small loss in the present in order to generate a larger gain or prevent a greater problem somewhere in the future. A person who cannot evaluate and manage himself objectively, a person who won't take a loss when it is required, regardless of how capable or knowledgeable he is in other areas, will eventually make a fatal error.

Current events are full of examples of highly intelligent people making public fools of themselves by not recognizing and dealing with difficult situations at a point in time when the damage from them is small and can be contained. Mistakes will be made, by you and by others. Take them in stride; deal with them wisely. As Robert Heinlein's character, Lazarus Long, says in the science fiction novel, *Time Enough for Love:* "The only cure for stupidity is death!" We might point out that objectivity and humility, while they may not cure stupidity, are effective antidotes. Use them regularly.

As a starting point for studying tactics, we will turn to the ancient Chinese again. Chinese oral tradition developed a set of ready-made tactics. These tactics, called *The Thirty-Six Stratagems,* are handed down from pre-history. We use the keyword S-W-O-R-D to help you remember the tactics so you can actually use them.

These ancient tactics have been handed down for thousands of years because they work. Using them effectively does indeed give you a S-W-O-R-D in hand. The great problem with employing *The Thirty-Six Stratagems* is that they are not easy to remember because they are usually presented in direct, literal translation from the original Chinese. The material we communicate here will be reworded for understanding and then related to applications and examples from Hold 'em and from various types of interpersonal transactions to help you remember them when they are needed.

To do this, we are going to divide the original thirty-six tactics into five groups, with six to eight tactics in each group, plus one tactic which stands alone because it does not belong in any particular group.

The five S-W-O-R-D groups are tactics based on:

Strength

Weakness

Opportunity

Replacement

Disguise

And, as mentioned above, there is one additional tactic which belongs in a group of its own.

PART FOUR: END GAME AND RESULTS

Success in competitive situations can be defined as accomplishing desired objectives as a result of strategies and tactics chosen. In Hold 'em, of course, the idea is to win money. In business, career, wealth, power, and relationship situations, there can be many other objectives, in addition to money. No matter what the objective, however, achieving desired results is the target and the measure of a satisfactory outcome.

The end game in Hold 'em is the turn card and the river card. After the flop has been exposed, the possible final value of hands in Hold 'em, both yours and those of remaining opponents, becomes more susceptible to reasonable estimate. Analysis of tactics for turn and river betting is similar to analysis of post-flop betting (which we cover in the kinetics section), so most of the discussion in Part Four, End Game and Results, centers around bluffing and avoiding mistakes.

Mistakes are the best avenue of advantage in any competitive situation. The competitor who makes the fewest mistakes generally wins the contest. One of the more costly mistakes in Texas Hold 'em is calling a river bet made by the opposition. Players, especially amateurs, do not risk sizable amounts on the river without justification. River bets are usually sincere. In Chapter 18, we present a short story to illustrate the danger.

Bluffing is a highly effective tactic for turning potential defeat into real victory. No one in their right mind assumes that every contest will be decided on the basis of which player has the best hand, or the most money, or the largest army. A good bluff is a form of deception. It is a deliberate lie designed to steal the pot or win the contest without having the best hand or the winning position. Bluffs are grounded in emotion. Emotion plays a large part in the ebb and flow of competition; fear, anger, greed, lust, and envy are the cornerstones of successful bluffing.

Using the keyword, S-E-A-L, we will analyze four out of the enormous number, variety, and combinations of different approaches to bluffing and deception that are available to persons involved in interpersonal competition.

The keyword S-E-A-L stands for:

Seduction

Enlistment

Assurance

Lying (the absolute favorite for poker players)

Last Words: The Five *ills of <u>No Limit</u>

No Limit is a simple, straightforward method of organizing strategy and tactics for winning in interpersonal competition, in addition to winning the game of Texas Hold 'em. At the center of this simple method are five *ills: **Will, Skill, Fill, Kill,** and **BILL.** To win in interpersonal competition and in Texas Hold 'em, your actions need to be governed by the first four *ills:

1. **Will** means you have the desire and commitment to accomplish the goals you have set.

2. **Skill** means you have acquired the knowledge and experience to master the game you have decided to play.

3. **Fill** means you get the cards you need to play your hand.

4. **Kill** means you have the confidence and heart required to risk your chips or to lay down your hand when required and appropriate.

In order to get away cleanly and enjoy your profits, you should consider the final keyword of the book—the fifth *ill, **BILL**—a strategy for squeezing yourself out of tight situations, whether at the card table or in personal competition. **BILL** works if you have the right stuff to use it.

Now it's time to shuffle up and deal!

2

Poker 101

The Concepts of Texas Hold 'Em Strategy

SO YOU'RE NEW to Texas Hold 'em Poker? Not a problem. Texas Hold 'em poker is by far the best poker game for a beginning player to learn. In sharp contrast to other poker games, for instance Omaha High/Low or Seven-Card Stud, which entail a great many more possibilities and probabilities, Hold 'em can be learned in a few minutes by anyone with an interest, and can be played *fairly* well with a few hours of practice.

There are probably over one hundred Texas Hold 'em books on the market, many of which provide an excellent introduction to the rules of the game and basic strategy. (For a short refresher course, read the very brief outline of a typical Hold 'em session in Appendix A.) There are also several fine Hold 'em computer software training programs available. Our advice, if you are a beginning player, is to thoroughly familiarize yourself with the elements of play and strategy before you sit down at the table in a casino. Playing Hold 'em for the first time in casinos like the Bellagio or Caesar's on the Strip in Vegas can be intimidating. Knowing rules and strategy helps you maintain your poise until you figure out that there are very few players at the table who are any smarter or more qualified than you are.

Once you understand the fundamental structure of the game, you can play Hold 'em almost anywhere. Hold 'em may be an easy game to learn, but it is certainly difficult to master. And, not surprisingly, the "mastering" part is what costs money.

In this section, we are going to give you some tips for keeping your "master's degree" expenses to a minimum. We will also begin to blend interpersonal competition ideas with Hold 'em strategy. To get you oriented in the right direction, we will draw you a M-A-P.

....

The keyword M-A-P stands for:

Mistakes

Audacity

Probabilities
....

Common Mistakes

1. CHANGING YOUR STARTING-HAND SELECTION

The power and value of effective starting-hand selection is something that must be learned at the very beginning of every poker journey. (Chapter 11 covers starting-hand concepts in detail.) Starting with card combinations that are appropriate to your table position (relative to the dealer button) and your risk profile is an absolutely essential requirement to winning in Hold 'em.

Every time you start a hand of poker, you're confronted with the same decision: Given all the variables I can measure or estimate, do the cards I hold create a positive expectation? If the answer is yes, play on. If the answer is no, you *must* wait for the next hand. There are 169 possible unique combinations of two cards for a standard 52-card deck. Every time you are dealt pocket cards in Hold 'em you will receive one of these 169 combinations. Depending on your playing style and table position, only about 25 to 35 percent of these combinations should be playable. That means you should sit out about 70 percent of the hands played.

Decision risk analysis for business, career, wealth, power, and relationship situations can be much more complex. There are always a startlingly large number of possibilities available and seemingly too little information and time to evaluate them all, or even a significant portion. Under these conditions, a sensible set of preconditions for selecting the types of deals and partners you will consider should serve as a buffer to personal involvement at levels of risk that are unnecessary or uncomfortable.

The exact preconditions you set in the business arena may be fuzzier than those relating to pocket cards in Hold 'em, but the requirement that you do not violate your own "starting hand philosophy" in midstream is probably more important when there are a significantly greater number of possibilities (as there are in a business setting). Determine your preconditions with respect to a particular situation and stay within those limits until you have had time (when you are no longer under the pressure of making a decision) to rethink your parameters.

In the course of a given session of Hold 'em, it is easy to give in to the urge to change your starting hand profile. Even the best starting hand sequence will fail to produce success on occasion or, what is perhaps even more serious, will succeed too well. When things are going badly, particularly when the neophytes at the table are winning big pots with improbable draws, you will start to question your own logic. When things are going great and you cannot lose, you will start to feel comfortable. The most common, and dangerous, response under either of these circumstances is to "loosen up," play a few more hands, expand a few limits, and skip a few safeguards. Do so at your peril.

2. MISREADING THE SITUATION

A fundamental truth underlying the game of poker (and business, too) is that everything is relative. It is unconditionally true that the relative strength of a given hand depends entirely on the situation. Understanding the nature of the situation you face is absolutely the first prerequisite to winning. Another critical aspect of the game is that people tend to become emotional during work and play and emotion filters reality.

In Hold 'em, perhaps even more than elsewhere, value is unquestionably in the eye of the beholder. We tend to see what we want to see. We want to believe what we think would be in our best interest to believe, whether it is in fact true or not. When the power of emotion (greed, anger, elation, desperation, jealousy, etc.), overrides common sense, you can and will misestimate the value of the cards you hold. Of course, nothing can prevent your occasionally misreading the situation. Sometimes you will be fooled by the fall of the cards. That is part of the game. Even the best players lose hands quite frequently. You will be wildly successful at Hold 'em if you can win 50 percent of the hands you take to showdown.

The key to developing your perceptive acumen is accurate observation. Watch the other players carefully and use every bit of understanding you have to assess what they are doing and thinking. Practice people watching and perception manipulation skills at every opportunity because they will pay big dividends. (Chapters 9 and 10 discuss people-watching concepts.)

But there is one person sitting with you at the table who always requires diligent and objective scrutiny. That person is you. Watch what you are doing! When your play becomes ragged around the edges, make sure it isn't because you are allowing emotion to color your view of reality. Keep working on solid, basic principles of good play, even when the cards are bad. Know your limits in terms of time, money, and the operations of chance (that is, winning or losing big). When you reach your limits, stop for awhile, perhaps by dropping out for a few hands, or maybe even quitting for the night. In a business situation, take whatever time you can to clear your head. Most misreads are preventable. Give yourself the best opportunity to win by taking a moment to breathe.

3. WEARING A BLIND-(NO)-FOLD

There are several theories about playing the blinds. You can pick the theory that suits your temperament. But during a given session, stick to the same one or you will have difficulty learning from your mistakes. Regardless of how you choose to play the blinds, however, it is important to realize that folding the blind because your hand does not meet specific playing criteria is not the same as throwing away your money. People talk about "protecting the blind." Consider protecting your money first. The blinds are a sunk cost. That is, once the bet has been placed on the table, it is not recoverable.

 Blinds are forced bets posted by (usually) two players to the left of the dealer. The blinds serve as an monetary inducement for players to enter the pot.

You cannot protect your blind because it is already gone. What you can do is throw good money after bad by playing any old hand just to show other players that you will not allow your blinds to be "stolen." The same reasoning also applies to bets made in later betting rounds. Never allow yourself to be drawn into betting more money on a hand than is justified by your playing strategy.

4. MISMANAGING YOUR STAKE
Cash flow is the life blood of any type of gamble, whether made at the casino or in the marketplace. Without cash, the best idea or the best strategy will fail. Preserve your cash.

The other side of this coin is the adage, "Scared money never wins." If you are too afraid of losing your money, or you do not have enough to afford the inevitable losses you will incur, then you must stop playing. The kind of bold, confident attitude required to win in any type of competitive arena cannot be maintained when fear of loss is not balanced by knowledge, experience, and courage. The middle of the road is best. Be afraid of loss, but not too much. Play at the table limits where you are most comfortable and confident.

Audacity
The Encarta dictionary defines *audacity* as: "Daring or willingness to challenge assumptions or conventions or tackle something difficult or dangerous."

Contrast the definition of audacity with the definition of *arrogance*: "A strong feeling of proud self-importance that is expressed by treating other people with contempt or disregard."

There is a considerable difference in attitude between the two words. And the right attitude marks the advanced player. Audacity implies boldness and daring combined with observation, cleverness, and restraint. Arrogance is boldness without regard for the competition or the consequences. Arrogance, while it can be intimidating to weaker players, is dangerous and self-defeating when dealing with those who are knowledgeable and experienced. Audacious people (i.e., bold and clever) eat arrogant people (i.e., bold and stupid) for lunch!

Further, arrogance is usually a façade to cover-up fear of failure. If you fear failure so greatly that you cannot deal effectively with others when faced with the very real possibility they will get the better of you occasionally, or even often, you should not play Hold 'em nor entertain ambitions of a dramatically successful business career. Risk entails loss and loss hurts. Learn to recover. Hit for average, not for power. You will still get your home runs, just fewer strike outs!

The foundation of audacity is patience. The core of patience is objectivity and humility. By objectivity and humility we are not implying in any way that you should be timid. Great players can sense timid players. Objectivity and humility mean you are open to learn from mistakes and willing to evaluate your play rationally.

Why is patience so easy to say but so hard to practice? In our experience, outcomes in life and in poker are based on a mix of factors. Sometimes skill prevails, sometimes chance prevails. It is possible to achieve a series of outcomes from your efforts that lead you to believe that you are totally inept, even though you are doing all the things you are supposed to do. It is hard not to lose confidence under those circumstances.

On the other hand, it is possible to achieve great outcomes even though you do everything wrong. (If you want to see this happen, play $2/$4 Limit Hold 'em at any casino in Vegas for a couple of days. Time and again, you will observe the other tourists sitting down and

playing almost every hand. For a time, some will seem to win continuously while making this most fundamental of mistakes.)

Again, developing patience is not the same as being timid. You
cannot be timid to play poker, especially for higher stakes. Even
when you experience several tough beats in a row and a series of
draws that do not materialize, you must continue to wager chips on
good hands. If the pot is raised a number of times and you hold a
good hand, you cannot flinch. Your knowledge of the odds and the
people involved verify your belief that the hand has the best chance
to win the pot.

Without patience you cannot become a successful poker player or
an effective business leader. Plainly and simply, a strong measure of
patience is an absolute. Without patience, the poker player and business person will be a loser.

Patience is always a relative term. How much patience is enough?
The answer is: as much as required by the circumstances. The
advanced player is willing to wait for hours, or in business, career,
wealth, power, and relationship situations, perhaps years. He will
wait for the right starting hand, in the right circumstance, and in the
right position. He will not only sit quietly, he will also not complain
like many players do. He knows the cards will come and so he is able
to wait. He does not piddle away his chips or resources trying to
make marginal hands work from disadvantageous positions.

The advanced player does not gripe about the dealer's inability to
deliver him a playable hand, or about how life is unfair when he gets
a bad beat. He simply waits for the drought to pass. Patience comes
before profit, and patience is the key to the passageway of advanced
levels of performance, both in poker and in business.

Becoming the best player, whatever game you play, is based on
finding and exploiting small edges. Once you have gained emotional
control, you have a huge edge. Having patience, you can exercise
solid hand selection without self-doubt. Poker is a game of skill
because it allows the careful player to develop edges and improve
continuously. Maybe it's only 1 or 2 percent at a time. It may not
seem like much, but as you grow and learn, you will discover more
techniques and add to your repertoire.

The ability to act confidently and audaciously is the greatest benefit of exploiting the advantages gained through patient observation and continuous self-study. You will discover a whole new way of interacting with the game and with the other players. See a little bit here, discover a bit more there, and you will soon astonish yourself as to how much you will be able to understand from the small hints people give off. Each breakthrough opens the door to higher levels of knowledge and ability. This is the way of long-term success.

Probabilities

One of the most widely held misunderstandings about the game of poker is that outcomes (i.e., winning or losing) are somehow governed by luck. Many people believe that, in some insidious or magical fashion, good luck is the cornerstone of success in the game. Expert poker play is no more about luck and magic than stock trading is about throwing darts to pick the next investment. Stock trading, like poker, is a highly risky activity, of course, and costly miscalculations do occur even for the best in the business. But in stock trading, as in poker, the point of the game is to minimize the effect of negative results caused by the operation of chance. Minimize your losses in order to win.

In order to discuss the operation of probability and chance effectively, we need to provide a few definitions. First, let's look at the terms themselves—*probability* and *chance*—which we will use interchangeably. In statistics, the probability or chance that a certain event or outcome will occur is calculated by taking the total number of times the specific outcome can occur and dividing by the total number of all outcomes possible.

For example, shuffle up a 52-card poker deck without looking at the cards. Set it on the table. What is the probability (or chance) that the first card on the pile is the ace of spades? That probability is calculated as follows: There is one ace of spades in the deck, so the number of times the outcome can occur is one. There are 52 cards in the deck, so the number of possible outcomes is 52. The probability, then, is 1/52 or 0.01923.

Now let's talk about the idea of *expected value*. What if I offered you $50 if the first card was the ace of spades? Say you had to put up $1. So, if the first card is the ace of spades you get $50. If it is not, I get $1. Would you be willing to take the bet? Your decision should be based on the expected value of the bet. Expected value is found by multiplying the payoff of the bet times the probability of winning the bet. The expected value of this bet then is the payoff of the bet ($50) times the probability of winning (0.01923, which we calculated above): $50 times 0.01923 equals $0.9615, or slightly less than $1 (the cost of the bet). If you made this bet with me repeatedly over a long period of time, eventually you would go broke because the expected value, or return, is less than the cost of the bet.

Every decision you make, no matter the venue, has an expected value. In economic terms, you will be financially successful in life if the cumulative expected value of your decisions exceeds the cumulative cost. This type of thinking is particularly relevant, not only to playing poker, but to making any type of business decision involving economic consequences. Every winning poker player understands the concept of expected value and applies it to every betting decision every time. We will further discuss the concept of expected value in Chapter 13.

Good players do calculate expected value intuitively based on a host of factors: the cards, players, position, etc. On occasion, the outcomes of betting decisions that ordinarily have positive expected values can, and will, be negative because chance does not operate evenly or exactly. For example, your pocket aces may get cracked (beaten) three or four times in a row in a given game. That does not change the fact that playing pocket aces aggressively has a long-term positive expected value.

The key to success in business, and in poker, is training yourself to assess situations accurately enough, using the information available, to gauge when your expected values are positive. At the bottom line, the core objective of this book is providing you with the tools to do this assessment in the moment, when and where you need to do it, with as much control over your emotions as you can muster.

In our opinion, the whole reason for developing yourself into a superior poker player is that the attitude-control skills, decision-analysis skills, and people-management skills required to play winning Hold 'em are the same skills that are *absolutely* needed in order to be a superior business, career, wealth, power, and relationship decision maker.

Every poker game is a concentrated slice of life. Playing a hand of poker is experiencing the essence of the thrill of risk, the sweet taste of success, the bile of failure. We believe this aspect of the game explains in part its popularity. If you take learning the game seriously, you will increase your chances of overall success in life.

In order to win over the long run, the concepts of probability and expected value must be kept in the back of your mind when you play. Bad luck occurs when you consistently ignore the rules of probability when making betting decisions.

There is one simple, basic, critical principle underlying all success. That principle is: playing decisions (poker, business, career, wealth, power, and relationship) must be made in light of expected values. Positive values should be bet; negative values folded. Any improvement in your ability to bet when you should bet, and to fold when you shouldn't bet, will improve your outcomes. In short, you will get luckier!

This ends your Poker 101 session. The set of concepts presented in the M-A-P (Mistakes, Audacity, and Probabilities) section should have given you an idea of the type of journey we intend to take you on. We will cover the details of playing and winning in the chapters that follow. Come along and raise your level of success at Hold 'em and at business, career, wealth, power, and relationships.

PART ONE

POSITION

In Part One, we focus on how to develop the character and attitude to succeed at Hold 'em and at business. We will discuss the role played by ego, confidence, logic, luck, and ambition. The goal is to describe how to develop the ideal character to succeed at poker, in the executive suite, the political office, or any other business, career, wealth, power, and relationship situation.

♠ ♣ ♥ ♦

3

Building Confidence

POKER AND BUSINESS both involve mastery of people skills. The essential ingredient for winning in either of these games is understanding and manipulating our own behavior and that of others for the purpose of reaching our goals. In business situations, technical ability, education, access to capital, etc., can leverage people skills, but, in the end, it is the person who inspires trust, loyalty, and support who wins. In poker, technical understanding, good cards, ample funding, etc., can win in the short run, but the person who wins in the long term is the person who best reads other players' strengths and weaknesses and is able to utilize them to his own advantage. Our ability to manage the impressions and expectations of associates and competitors over a period of time ultimately determines how far we are able to progress. The P-O-W-E-R to manipulate impressions and to channel expectations begins with confidence.

Confidence is most certainly an internal state of mind, but confidence, or lack thereof, is readily visible in the way people behave.

Posture, movements, eyes, and voice continuously transmit highly reliable information about personal levels of comfort and confidence to others in the vicinity who have the ability to read the information. A critical first step toward improving success in business and in Texas Hold 'em is creating and nurturing confidence in our own abilities and in our approach to playing and working. Confidence can be enhanced using a logical process. We will use the keyword P-O-W-E-R to illustrate principles of building confidence.

··

The actions represented in the keyword P-O-W-E-R are:

Prepare

Organize

Weld

Experiment

Reward

··

P-O-W-E-R

PREPARE TO CHOOSE

A key initial action required to begin a process of improvement in your life is choosing the eventual outcome you desire. In other words, before you begin the process of improvement, you should choose the objective to be gained, something you want strongly enough to warrant going through the work required to move up the ladder in business and in society. To make an appropriate choice for yourself, it is necessary for you to be familiar with the alternatives available. You must "prepare" to choose.

Much of how a person organizes reality has been picked up or absorbed, mostly without conscious evaluation, through cultural, educational, and social experience. For better or worse, we tend to believe and use attitudes, methods, and biases we receive from those around us. Choices are made for us through association and chance, without our being presented with enough information to choose for ourselves. Informed choice requires information. Get the best information available and make your own carefully considered choice of direction and goals.

In Hold 'em, there are probably three levels of choice to be made. We bring this subject up here because in the opinion of many Hold 'em experts a person ends up playing more successfully if he specializes in a specific structure, type of game, and stakes level. As you play, you should begin considering which combination of alternatives are the most comfortable for your style, commitment, and budget. The three levels of choice are:

1. Which structure of game to play (for a description of Limit versus No Limit, see Appendix A)

2. Which type of game (cash or tournament)

3. How high the level of stakes to risk (from nothing except time to everything you've got)

There are essential differences among the three alternatives. Very briefly (because you should experiment with different games to find out for yourself), Limit Hold 'em is a much more methodical game than No Limit. Success in Limit depends more on patience, while success in No Limit depends upon timing your moves.

Cash games are far less time and resource constrained than tournaments; there is no reason in a cash game for playing out of position or with bad cards, while tournament structure may require less than optimal play.

Finally, playing the level of stakes that is in tune with your financial comfort levels will greatly enhance your ability to make those critical raise, call, or fold decisions objectively.

ORGANIZE FACTS

Amorphous masses of data and facts are not useful to the decision process. Data and facts must be organized before they can be called information and used to make rational decisions. During your data-gathering efforts, take a moment to think about your priorities. Some things will be more important than others in reaching your goals. Organize facts around priorities. Point yourself in the direction of your desires; you are more likely to succeed as a result.

Decisions are the key element in winning. Better decisions yield better results. Hold 'em decisions are almost always based on incomplete information. As a consequence, some kind of decision process will be employed to filter partial information and arrive at course of action. Most people have not actually evaluated the decision process they employ. Take a minute and think through your own decision process. It's something that probably "just happened" without deliberate choice on your part. Improving decisions begins with improving the process used.

At the very least, in order to be useful, an effective decision process needs to be structured. Here is a suggestion for structuring decisions which you can use as a starting point.

Imagine for a moment that you are standing on the deck of a sleek sailing ship traveling across a beautiful blue lake. There is a gentle breeze and you are clipping along. Look at the sails. They are filled with wind and drive the ship in the desired direction.

Now look at the *mast*. The purpose of the mast is to transmit the force of wind to the body of the ship. The mast itself provides no motive power, but serves as the all-important conduit for the power of the wind. For the purpose of analogy, assume that wind is the information you gather. Information tells you which way the wind is blowing and determines how you must tack and steer in order get where you want to go. The mast is your decision process.

··
The actions represented in the keyword M-A-S-T are:

Measure

Analyze

Synthesize

Test
··

Measure means thinking about your information in terms that can be expressed with numbers. Some examples are: How much? How high? What cost? What are the pot odds? What is my position? How many times has a particular player raised? Ask specific questions related to the decision at hand and express those questions in terms that can be measured in some fashion.

Analyze means providing a series of answers to your questions and assessing how reliable those answers might be. As you ask questions in the measure phase, create answers that are specific within the context of the decision situation.

Synthesize means developing the consequences of your analyze phase. What does it mean that the player who is raising before the flop has only played three out of fifty hands dealt? In the synthesize phase, develop your working hypothesis, make a decision, and evolve a course of action.

Test means acting on your decision, implementing your course of action and, especially, evaluating the results. You will feed back the results of the current decision into the decision process in order to make better decisions in the future.

WELD TO WIELD

If you intend to create a tool out of scraps of metal, you need to *weld* them together before they will be useful in improving your results. *Weld* here refers to the process of placing ideas in your mind in such a way that they are readily accessible when needed. This book will present you with literally hundreds of ideas and concepts, mostly in the form of keywords or other mnemonic phrases, which have been crafted specifically to aid you in competitive situations. But unless you have a great deal of time and energy, you will not remember much of what you read unless and until you commit a phrase or two to memory.

There is, of course, no way you can take the time to memorize all the items presented here. Our suggestion, then, for welding concepts into your memory is to select two or three keywords and begin to use them in your daily routine. If you recall from school, the best method to learn a new vocabulary word is to use it three times in one day. The same approach applies to these keywords. If you will use a specific keyword a few times each day for a week or so, it will weld itself in your memory sufficiently well to be useful in times of need.

EXPERIMENT TO EVOLVE

The concepts put forth in this book become static once they are written down. That is, they are presented as fixed principles. Unfortunately, the situations we tend to get involved with in real life are anything but static. Circumstances involved in business, career, wealth, power, and relationship decisions are always uncertain; many situations, if not most, are chaotic.

As in Hold 'em, challenges in life are rarely resolved until the river card is dealt. Your opponent always seems to have a few *outs* that will defeat you. Further, as in Hold 'em, using a static approach to overcoming challenges almost guarantees losing because experienced opponents will quickly read your strategies and counter them. Hence, it is particularly important to evolve your strategy and tactics over time.

 An "out" is a card that improves the value of a hand to the point where it can win the pot.

Evolution requires experimentation; there is no other way. But in order to experiment, you must have a starting point. You should initially select what seems to you to be the most appropriate approach to winning considering your individual appetites, objectives, personality, and style. We will present an array of considerations throughout this book, but making a firm decision to select an approach and then acting decisively on that choice is a primary and necessary beginning to your success. Every expert, every champion, every winner began to succeed when he made a firm decision about how to approach his own development.

Once you have created a starting point, watch and consider carefully what happens. Take the time to evaluate results, and then experiment with alternative methods and tactics. Use the M-A-S-T technique described above. Follow your own success. Continue doing things that seem to be working for you; and, even more importantly, stop doing things that are not working for you (regardless of whether they work for others). Confidence is born from success, not failure. If you win, you will consider yourself a winner. Make sure that happens by following a path that results in positive and meaningful outcomes for you.

These ideas are particularly important in playing Hold 'em. There are a large variety of approaches to winning the game. All of these approaches can be traced back to a small set of sound playing fundamentals, but the way these fundamentals are applied varies dramatically among the better players. In business as in Hold 'em, master the fundamentals first, but apply the techniques in accordance with methods and styles that work for you. Choose a starting point; pay attention to your results; modify your methods; follow your success.

REWARD TO REMEMBER

The final aspect in developing the P-O-W-E-R of confidence is rewarding yourself for remembering to do what you have chosen to do. Just making a decision to do something a different way is not sufficient to effect change for most people. It is like making a New Year's resolution. Making the resolution is easy. Making the change required is difficult. All people respond to rewards. If it is your choice to adopt a new or different approach, reward yourself for success.

It is very easy for people who care about the results of their actions to be critical of their own failures. This is another reason why Hold 'em is an excellent vehicle for teaching oneself to succeed. Most of the time you do not succeed at Hold 'em. What we mean here is not that you will lose in the long-term, but that most of the time you are playing in a game, you are watching someone else play. Most of the hands you are dealt are not (or should not be) playable. Those that are playable often bust out on the flop. Those you decide to play because you get a piece of the flop (or in spite of not getting a piece, as the case may be) are often beaten on the turn or river. Short-term failure occurs much more often than success in Hold 'em. To win at Hold 'em, you must have a high tolerance for failure.

This is not to say you accept failure. You can be a bad loser if you want to be (try to be civil though.) It is critical, however, that you celebrate success. When you do what you expect of yourself, give yourself a pat on the back. Most of the time no one else will do it for you. Take care of your ego. Give yourself a present. Winners believe in themselves, and part of the reason they win is because they believe they will.

The ultimate level of success you achieve in Texas Hold 'em and in business will depend in part on how well you are able to manipulate your own behavior and the behavior of others. If you learn to control and train your own behavior, you will have taken the absolutely essential first step to being able to influence the behavior of others. Confidence is born out of the choice to manage yourself and the P-O-W-E-R that flows from that choice.

♠ ♣ ♡ ◇

4

Anger, Frustration, and Fear

IN CHAPTER 3, we talked about establishing confidence by deciding on a set of objectives and developing a plan of action to achieve those objectives. A sense of confidence combined with feelings of power and commitment can provide, at the very least, the beginnings of progress in interpersonal competition. And, without a doubt, confidence is an essential element for success in Texas Hold 'em. But day-to-day existence is filled with anxiety, worry, and challenge. Every person who is actively engaged in trying to manage his position in the marketplace, or trying to win pots in Hold 'em, feels anger, frustration, and fear to varying degrees almost constantly. The key to achievement in the long term is your ability to make anger, frustration, and fear work for you and against your competitors.

The nature of our response to tough situations has been developed through experience and observation reaching back to the very beginnings of our lives. What we do when we are afraid or challenged is deeply rooted in our character. Further, most of the programming for these influential aspects of our lives was completed before we could make any rational choice about how to act under stress and what type of response was really appropriate for us. As a consequence, there are deeply ingrained traits in each of us, traits that present themselves in response to thorny circumstances, traits we have accepted at the very deepest levels, which may not produce effective results. In order to win, we must identify and use both positive and negative character traits in ourselves and others. This is critically important for those traits that can be problematic when the chips are down.

The Five Character Flaws

In *The Art of War,* Chinese general and philosopher Sun Tzu identifies five critical character flaws that can be employed to defeat a competitor:

1. Recklessness

2. Anxiety

3. Timidity

4. Short-temperedness

5. Self-importance

Sun Tzu not only advises us to use these traits against opponents, but also to eliminate them from ourselves. *If you take nothing else away from this book in your pursuit of success in Hold 'em or in business, career, wealth, power, and relationship contests, remember these five character flaws.* To the extent you are able to control your own negative outcomes from these traits, and to the extent you encourage and manage the negative reactions of others, you will greatly improve your odds of winning.

Much of what is being covered here may be considered blatantly manipulative. We make no excuse or apology for this. In an ideal world, higher concepts of teamwork, cooperation, and enlightened relationships would prevail. Unfortunately, we live in a chaotic, competitive, and downright dangerous world.

Manipulation is employed in every possible way and in every aspect of living. You must master both the higher concepts of competition and management and the lower concepts (if you would consider manipulation to be part of the "lower" concepts), to achieve anything worthwhile in the long run. If you do not, you will most certainly be defeated by someone who did learn to use them. Manipulation is a tool like anything else. How the tool is used depends upon the purposes and character of the individual using it.

The keyword for the five character flaws identified by Sun Tzu is R-A-T-S-S.

··
The traits represented by the keyword <u>R-A-T-S-S</u> are:
Reckless
Anxious
Timid
Short-Tempered
Self-Important
··

You can easily see that identifying these traits in your fellow Hold 'em players enhances your advantage in the game. Under the pressure of play, opponents can display negative traits very quickly. The idea here would be to put the other players on tilt, if possible, by using their particular character flaws against them. Beware of your own propensities in the process though. Good players can turn the tables.

In a professional business environment, identifying character flaws does not necessarily lead to an immediate opportunity to create an advantage. Dealing with seriously flawed individuals in positions of power or influence can be tricky at best. Sometimes it is better to allow time to pass and perhaps the person will self-destruct. On the other hand, it is extremely important, if you are in a position of power, to avoid promoting or supporting those around you who display flaws openly. They can be dangerous to you.

Subtlety in dealing with competitors and associates is always more desirable than being heavy-handed. Hold your observations about others in confidence. Use the knowledge you glean sparingly. The reason for this is twofold. First, any negative comment that you make about an associate in the business setting will almost certainly be repeated and eventually make its way back to the subject of your comment. Second, loyalty and trustworthiness are two of the most highly prized (by superiors especially) attributes for an employee or executive to possess. Negative opinions, even though voiced in reference to persons who are perhaps deserving of them, lowers your loyalty and trustworthiness score. You do not want to be known as a really smart and talented person who has negative opinions about others. Keep them hidden.

The same is true at the Hold 'em table. You will seldom go very long in a session before someone has something negative to say about another player, about the cards, about the casino, about the dealer, or about some other aspect of the game. Be sociable, but hold your criticism at the table.

This is particularly true when it comes to differences of opinion where money is concerned. The most common of these, in our experience, is an argument about whether a player made the correct bet or put in the correct blind. Let the dealer or floor manager decide. Even if you think you know what happened and are asked for an opinion, for your own good, stay out of it. If you want to see an excellent example of how ugly things can get, watch a tape of the argument between poker pros Jeff Lisandro and Prahlad Freidman about a missing $5,000 blind chip in 2006 World Series of Poker main event.

Here is what Sun Tzu has to say about the five character flaws (R-A-T-S-S):

Reckless

If an opponent is reckless, we can cause him to waste his resources.

Anxious

If an opponent is overly concerned about his level of skill or about losing money, he will vacillate when making a difficult decision at a critical moment.

Timid

If an opponent is timid, we can usurp his resources (steal his bets or blinds).

Short-Tempered

If an opponent is short-tempered, we can cause him to be rash and defeat himself.

Self-Important

If an opponent is self-important, we can distract him with flattery and appeals to his superiority.

Each of these character flaws can be used to leverage competitors and associates when time and circumstances permit. (We will often mention the critical importance of recognizing appropriate circumstances and employing effective timing with regard to successfully executing any kind of plan, strategy, or tactic. No strategy or tactic is infallible. Consideration of situation and timing are essential to any kind of success.)

Most individuals have some idea of their flaws; many are (unwisely, we might add) very proud of them. If you are obviously playing to someone's weakness, they may be quite aware of what you are doing and be fairly good at defending themselves, and possibly even retaliating against you (flawed individuals tend to be tough and nasty or they would not have survived). More importantly, excellent players will simulate weakness in order to induce overconfidence, predictability, and carelessness in the other players.

Simulating weakness is especially common among excellent Hold 'em players. Setting a trap in Hold 'em almost always depends on creating some type of false impression, usually false weakness. Think about your plan carefully when your opponent seems to be oblivious to it and winning appears easy. The majority of your opponents are not stupid when it comes to self-preservation.

Character of a C-H-A-M-P

If you want to help your chances for future success in both Hold 'em and your career, you should be asking yourself whether you do indeed display some (or all, at various times) of the five character flaws. The answer for the very great majority of us is: Yes! (If you can honestly say "No," put this book down and figure out how to run for Congress, because lying to yourself and believing it is an absolute primary skill needed for holding office.) The real issue is not whether you do now, or did, at some point in your history, display these flaws, but whether you recognize them and are willing to attempt to self-manage your behavior.

Managing behavior with regard to the weaknesses discussed (and others you may identify) is not an option if you want better than average results out of life and out of poker. It is essential to shield yourself from being outplayed by other people who know how to use simple tactics designed to leverage your obvious flaws into big mistakes. Smart players in interpersonal competition and in the casino will quickly and effectively employ these tactics against you (and, of course, at the very least, even if they win, you want to make them work hard to beat you).

To structure our suggestions for mitigating the five character flaws, we are using the keyword C-H-A-M-P.

....

The character traits represented by the keyword C-H-A-M-P are:

Courage

Humility

Approach

Means and Methods

Product

....

COURAGE

Our working definition of *courage* is the ability to take constructive action in the face of realized adversity or challenge. It is difficult to manage or modify one's own behavior. Courage is needed in order to recognize the need to try. Courage is also required to stand back up when you do not reach your goals. People who display courage are less apt to be timid or anxious, but perhaps a little more prone to recklessness.

HUMILITY

Humility means the ability to set aside one's personal world view in the face of reality. Seeing things as they are, and not as you would want them to be, requires dampening the voice of ego. Humility definitely does not mean backing down in the face of a challenge. It means facing the challenge with your eyes open. Carrying humility too far may lead to vacillation.

APPROACH

There is a line from a Celine Dion song that says: "Life is what happens while you are making other plans." *Approach* here relates to keeping your mind flexible. Change is constant. Good plans at one point in time can be total disasters at another. When you approach planning and managing difficult situations with flexibility, humility, and courage, you are far less likely to lose sight of reality. Reactions are based on objective analysis and careful consideration. Further, you are also less apt to lose your temper and go on tilt when outcomes do not conform to desires, which is, of course, most of the time.

MEANS AND METHODS

Employ *means and methods* that are effective and reasonable given the task, challenge, or goal at hand. Many goals take a long time to realize, and often the outcome is in doubt until the very end. Judge carefully how much and where to apply effort and resources. The level of risk you are taking at a given point determines to a great extent how much you have left to reinvest later.

Guard time and assets. Investing too much of either in the wrong situation can reduce your capacity to bet on the next opportunity. New opportunities arise every time a card is turned. As a result, folding bad positions early, particularly in the face of intense opposition or great uncertainty, is almost never an irrevocable error. Put yourself in a position to maintain a workable level of flexibility. Balance risk against reward.

PRODUCT

Reaching a desirable outcome is the objective. No one will care how much time or money you spent, no one will care how smart you are or how hard you worked if you cannot produce desirable results. Set ego aside, to a reasonable extent, and focus attention on the end *product*. Under most circumstances, you will not suffer if you can show real accomplishment or be a recognized member of the winning side.

Bad Beats

Bad beats are a major cause of frustration and anger. Let's take a minute and formulate a reasonable definition of a bad beat. For the purposes of discussion and in the context of Texas Hold 'em, a *bad beat* occurs whenever the underdog in a heads-up confrontation wins after being behind by at least 3 to 1 at some point in the hand; that is, the underdog had at some point 25 percent or less chance of winning the hand. A 3 to 1 underdog will win 25 percent of the time. (More on odds calculation in Chapter 5, so bear with us if you are a little rusty in this area of math.)

 In Hold 'em, a common "bad beat" occurs when a lower pair beats a higher pair by drawing a set. (A "set" is three of a kind comprised of a pocket pair and one matching ranked card on the board. "Trips," on the other hand, are three of a kind comprised of one pocket card with two on the board.) The odds of a lower pair beating a higher pair, heads-up, are about 4 to 1.

Even though you may recognize that bad beats are a common aspect of the game, there is no antidote to the wave of helplessness and futility that accompanies the realization that you have been put out of a tournament by someone who had two outs on the river. The greatest difference between an amateur and a professional, at the poker table and elsewhere, is the ability to take a bad beat and continue to perform at a high level.

Bad beats happen to good players and bad players alike. Don't let your experience in the last hand, or last job, or last marriage, ruin your chances of success in the present. Learn to control your anger, frustration, and fear.

♠ ♣ ♡ ◇

5

The Role of Luck

LIFE ON THE MATERIAL plane, life in this world we have, life in the midst of this reality, is all about winning the game. It's not about playing well and losing. Not about being a good sport and kissing someone else's behind while they stroll down victory lane. Joy, delight, profit, and happiness are all found in victory. And victory is sweet, especially at the poker table.

Unfortunately, winning and losing, the final outcomes of our cumulative efforts, are ultimately determined by luck, or fortune, or fate, or God's will, or whatever you wish to call it. Luck pervades everything we do. We can never, ever, even for a moment, eliminate the impact of luck on our ultimate fate, nor predict its direction. You might as well get used to it!

Our only hope is to enthusiastically embrace the uncertainty and chaos as it passes and hang on for dear life as it hurls us into whatever future lies over the next horizon. This book is about developing the ability to perceive the reality of the chaos all around us, about learning to accept it, and about gaining the wisdom to manage your relationship to it. Where chaos takes you, what it does to you, how long you travel, what you see and do on the way, and who you become in the end . . . well, those are your challenges. Better savor the trip, though, because it's all you've got to work with in this lifetime.

Having said all that, why not just throw the book away and take our chances with luck? Studying the lives and actions of successful people throughout history in every field of work—military, science, business, politics, etc.—shows us that ultimate victory may come from a single flash of genius or one critical moment of inspired decision. However, the people who succeed have generally spent years preparing for that flash or that decision, developing the skills and attitudes that tend to invite success.

If you want to get struck by lightning, you need to be walking around outside during thunderstorms. Hiding in closets won't help. Encourage positive things to happen for you by employing the same methods that successful people have been using since the human race walked out of Africa 100,000 years ago; that is, do it the hard way. You have no guarantees, but if you want to hit a home run in the World Series, you have to the play the game very well.

H-A-R-D W-A-Y

Doing things the hard way encourages luck to show up and help you. Maybe it's the fickle nature of the universe, but success seems to like people who do things the hard way.

The actions represented by the keyword H-A-R-D W-A-Y are:

Handle the Cards

Ask the Tough Questions

Reduce the Field

Develop Constancy

Wait and Watch

Angle for Advantage

Yes! Say "Yes!"

HANDLE THE CARDS

At the time you are reading these words, you may find yourself in a position where you have a limited field of authority to take action on your own initiative. If you are working for a company as an employee or contractor, your authority will always be limited within the context of your task and objectives. Even when you are top dog, you will have to operate within the constraints of maintaining some level of profitability and satisfying customer objectives—however "customer" may be defined for your given activity. Virtually no one has unlimited freedom of action.

Although you may not act independently on a wide range of issues, take advantage of every opportunity to control what you can control within the scope of your responsibility. Think through what you should and could do to better satisfy the needs of the people you interact with. People who satisfy needs find success. When you handle the cards, you improve your opportunity to tip circumstances in your favor, thereby increasing the probability of a favorable outcome.

ASK THE TOUGH QUESTIONS

People lie. Oh yeah, they do. All the time. When asked for an explanation, the average person will generally provide that version of the truth that best enhances his personal position or pocketbook. You simply cannot afford to accept the explanations of others at face value. You will need to dig out the truth. Ask tough questions if you want answers you can depend upon. Further, expect everything but the truth in response: evasion, anger, tap dancing, and outright fabrication.

Of course, these considerations in no way impugn the reliability and morality of the average person, particularly the average Hold 'em player. You can bet that whatever reliability or morality the average person possesses is confined to situations that best suit his own personal interests. Do not trust *your* plans or conclusions to their veracity. Ask again. Ask the same thing in a different way. Cross-check with alternative sources. Do a smell test (does the answer smell right?) Does the hand your opponent is representing make sense in the context of the board and his previous bets? If others get angry or disturbed at your repeated inquiries, they are either lying or stupid. Protect your own interests well.

Because success is based on rational and accurate analysis of reality, you must be careful to question yourself, too. Ask yourself: Why am I doing this? What do I have to gain? Whom will I hurt or benefit? Am I doing this because my mother, father, sister, brother, lover, etc., wants it done? Does this make sense? Do I have alternatives? You can be your own worst enemy. Take pains to mitigate the harm you do to yourself by challenging your own conclusions when they entail serious consequences.

REDUCE THE FIELD

The principle suggested here is this: The fewer the number of competitors in a contest, the greater the chance each one has to win. You will apply this principle over and over in Hold 'em. For instance, when holding higher middle pairs (99,TT), if you are first to act, you may want to raise the pot enough to drive out marginal hands before the flop. Other than the fact that 99 and TT are made hands, and, as a result, beat any unpaired holding, these hands are not particularly strong against a larger group of competitors. Reducing the field improves your chances a great deal.

When making a move to reduce the field, minimize the risk to yourself and your own prospects. On a personal level (such as office politics), indirect moves that focus on reducing the confidence of competitors can work well and remain hidden. That is, look for ways to reduce your competitors' confidence in themselves or the confidence their associates and superiors have in them.

A subtle "smear campaign" (to call it what it is), which cannot be traced back to you personally, is an effective tactic. Negative comments travel very quickly and efficiently through the grapevine (as opposed to positive comments, which few people really care about). Dropping negative information in appropriately chosen venues can wreak havoc with someone else's perceived value. But watch out for the backdraft.

The parallel in Hold 'em is putting a strong beat on someone at the table through a trap play. Most obviously, this *might* be accomplished by slow-playing pocket aces or kings (but try this very carefully). If you are able to surprise someone out of a large pot, other players tend to become wary of your trapping them too. You will rattle their confidence a little, giving you a bit of an advantage when you do not have a super hand to start with.

DEVELOP CONSTANCY

The type of constancy we are referring to here is constancy of purpose and evenness of temperament. We have noted previously that constancy of method or constancy of approach to specific situations, such as certain Hold 'em hands, allows others to script you. If your opponents can script you, they can defeat you. Constancy of purpose and evenness of temperament prevent permanent harm from the gut-wrenching swings of emotion you can (and will) experience during the inevitable ups and downs associated with competing for a higher level of achievement in life.

Constancy of purpose gives you the ability to view the successes and failures you meet on the road of progress through the moderating lens of objectivity. You know where you are going; you have a solid, defined endpoint in mind. The way to that endpoint may not be a straight line; however, a clear vision of the future, combined with the will to succeed, can carry you through the curves and over the bumps.

WAIT AND WATCH

Patience is always the distinguishing mark of an accomplished Hold 'em player. Patience accompanied by attentive observation is a powerful combination. Study the way big cats hunts their prey. First, they mark out a target animal (usually a weaker member of the group they are stalking). Next, they wait and watch until a moment arrives when they believe they have an advantage. Finally, they strike with intent to kill.

One important characteristic of all successful predators is that they do not attack unless they believe they have an advantage. A successful predator cannot afford to be hurt by its prey. If hurt, the predator cannot hunt or defend itself, and its survival becomes questionable.

Successful predators avoid fair fights and even-up matches whenever possible because their outcomes are in doubt.

Smart lions do not pick on the biggest antelope in the herd because they want to show the other lions they are "the man" (or "the top cat," as the case may be.) They are perfectly content snacking on the weak, the tired, the lame, and the unwary—where the risk of injury is very low and the probability of success very high. Be a lion, not a donkey!

ANGLE FOR ADVANTAGE

Let's expand the predator metaphor a little farther. What do lions do while they are waiting for the chance to attack their lunch? Do they wander over to the nearest tree and lay down? Maybe a juicy antelope or a tasty zebra or a delicious donkey will just stroll by. Even lions know all things come to those who wait, don't they?

Actually, all things come to those who work like hell when they are waiting. Lions do know this. A hunting lioness will constantly maneuver, in concert with her companions, to isolate and control the movement of the target animals. She will seek every chance to gain a small advantage for herself. Accumulating small advantages adds up to large benefits eventually. While you are waiting for your chance at fame and fortune, or while you are waiting for pocket rockets (two Aces) in Hold 'em, work to accumulate any advantage and every chip you can.

YES! SAY "YES!"

Opportunity comes to each and every one of us. Life dispenses opportunity, just like it deals good hands, in equal measure in the long-run. (If you think this is stupid optimism, why did you buy this book?) Opportunities may not be obvious, nor do they always present themselves as uplifting, stimulating challenges (most opportunities disguise themselves as difficult and boring tasks), but opportunities arise all the time nonetheless. The problem is that we are not accustomed to welcoming them. Unless you are willing to *consider* opening the door when opportunity knocks, eventually you will not hear it, even if it is pounding away on your front porch.

Say "yes" once in a while when an item or situation comes along that tempts your fancy or tickles your interest. Nothing ever looks like a sure thing unless you are seeing it in the rearview mirror. Testing and considering opportunities trains the mind to think through how they might succeed for us. As we noted above, the road of progress is neither straight nor smooth. But, you can make an unplanned left hand turn once every so often. You can bluff a little. You can start with a 67 off-suit sometimes. You may be surprised at where you end up. (Or you may be dismayed, obviously. Don't pitch caution out the window. That only works in movies.)

Throw Away the S-P-A-D-E!

The spade we are talking about is the one you use to dig a hole and bury yourself while playing Texas Hold 'em. If you want to get lucky at poker, the first thing you need to do is stop putting yourself in the position to be unlucky. Using the experience of over 1,000 tournaments and over 1 million hands dealt (among the perpetrators of this book), we have postulated these five short rules to help you stay out of troublesome situations where you can experience bad beats and other unpleasant consequences.

··

The keyword we use here is S-P-A-D-E, which stands for:

Starting Hands

Pairs

Aces

Drawing Hands

Ego Calls

··

STARTING HANDS

Unless you have the poker skills of a Gus Hansen or Daniel Negreanu, you may want to consider limiting your starting hands to those that have a fairly high probability of ending up part of a winning combination. The starting hand is the foundation for all the possible groups of cards forming the poker hands that you can utilize to win. As we discussed in Chapter 2, a high proportion of possible starting hands (maybe 65 to 75 percent of the 169 possible starting hands) have little chance to generate a winning hand. Leave them alone, for your own good. Pick a set of starting hands that works for you and stick with it except for that rare situation where you want to try something foolish for fun.

Starting with potentially valuable hole cards is a piece of advice you will get in every poker book you read. Everyone knows about starting hands. Yet in game after game, tournament after tournament, we see people (and thankfully, we might add) who play almost every hand even when holding absolute garbage. Starting with an extremely wide range of hands does not, *in and of itself*, create a large number of profitable opportunities to trap or outplay other players. Think about it.

Using sound judgment with starting hands is even more critical when calling a raise. The standard (and really wise) advice is: Do not call a raise unless you have at least a hand you could have raised with from your position; preferably, the hand should be a little better. Even though you may want to believe that everyone bluff-raises from early position, most of us do not. Let the weaker hands go, pick up some luck, save some chips.

PAIRS

For purpose of discussion and analysis, we will divide pairs into three major groups:

1. Micro-pairs (22, 33, and 44)

2. Mid-pairs (55 to JJ)

3. Macro-pairs (QQ, KK, and AA)

Mid-pairs are further divided into two subgroups:

Low mid-pairs (55, 66, 77, and 88)

High mid-pairs (99, TT, and JJ)

Memorize these groupings to get the ranking and terminology fixed in your mind.

A pair is a made hand. As such, it beats any hand containing only high cards, such as AK or AQ. In a *heads-up,* all-in showdown situation, a pair has an ever-so-slight advantage over these high-card hands (about 55 percent to 45 percent). However, based on computer simulation, pairs are the winning hand no more than half the time when they are not improved by the flop, turn, or river. Hence, pairs are a weak bet in the long-run. Pocket pairs will improve by the river to three of a kind only about 1 out of 5 tries (20 percent of the time).

 "Heads-up" is a pot that is contested by only two players.

Our conclusion is that playing pocket micro-pairs or mid-pairs too strongly, particularly going all-in before the flop, is unwise and invites bad luck. Consider soft-playing these hands, and even folding to overcards on the flop. Of course, in the process you will throw away some winning hands. However, trapping other players with a flopped set can become more profitable. If you do not frequently showdown micro-pairs and mid-pairs, others will give a lower probability to your playing them. This will allow you to profit more often from a trips-trap.

 An "overcard" is a card higher than any card on the board.

ACES

People love to play aces, and with good reason. Even a lowly A2 off-suit wins 55 percent of the time against a random hand. Playing Ax indiscriminately, however, leads to disaster, particularly if your ace does not pair on the flop. In a nutshell, don't chase the ace.

Let us reemphasize that point: *Do not chase the ace.* If you are looking at an unpaired Ax after the flop, you have 6 outs to pair one or the other card, which is about 24 percent on turn and 12 percent on river. Yet many players will go all the way to the river holding just an unpaired ace. Save your chips. Consider folding.

DRAWING HANDS

Effectively managing draws is a cornerstone of Hold 'em success. We will go into the mathematics and tactics of drawing hands later in the book. This section is concerned with going all-in after the flop holding a drawing hand like AK or AQ.

AK and AQ are powerful combinations before the flop and are certainly worthy of strong betting. But these powerful hands are drawing hands; any pair beats them. After the flop, if you have not paired one of your cards (or better), think carefully before initiating or calling an all-in.

A drawing hand, no matter how strong, is just that. It is less of a mistake to fold to a bluff (which will happen seldom, particularly in early and middle stages of a tournament) than to get bounced out of a tournament by a pair of 2s. Beware the draw after the flop.

EGO CALLS

Let's create a hypothetical situation. You are holding AK (diamonds) in the pocket. The flop comes three small diamonds (3, 5, 9). You have flopped a *nut flush*.

Your dream flop has arrived. You bet heavily. The person in the big blind is the only player who calls your bet. The turn comes J (clubs). You bet again. The big blind smooth calls again. He is so beaten. What a donkey! Your mouth waters; you are already counting the chips in the pot. The river comes a 5 (spades). You bet again. The big blind goes all-in. What the heck is he doing? No way he can have a boat (that is, a full house). No way. Must be trying to push two pair or be plain bluffing. Must be. Your ego is screaming, "You are stupid to lay down such a wonderful hand." So you call. The big blind lays down 99 for nines full of fives. You are dead!

 The "nuts" is the best possible hand, given the board. The best possible straight or flush is the "nut straight" or "nut flush."

Granted, it would be difficult for anyone to lay down a nut flush on the river. It has been our experience, however, in an overwhelming number of cases, that if someone places a big bet on the river, he generally has something close to the nuts. Gaining the discipline to lay down hands that are probably beaten, despite the screams and protests of your ego, will decrease "bad beats" and increase profit.

We started this chapter by suggesting that there was little you could do about the fact that luck influences the outcomes in your life. There is a great deal you can do, however, to encourage good luck and discourage bad luck. Make the most of the chances you get.

♤ ♧ ♡ ♢

6

Using Logic to Make Good Decisions

STRONG LOGIC precedes good luck, at least some of the time. Luck, good or bad, has to do with the consequences of decisions. Logic, strong or weak, has to do with analyzing situations and developing decisions. The stronger and more relevant the logic being applied to crafting a given decision, the more favorable the consequences of that decision are likely to become. Good logic can never overcome bad luck as a determinant of outcome; bad luck will beat you every time. But bad luck appears much more frequently as a consequence of action when weak logic has been applied during the analysis and decision-making process.

Success in Texas Hold 'em and advancement in business and career both involve making effective decisions and correct choices under conditions of uncertainty. A person never has all the information available when making a choice. However, by using strong and effective logic in selecting one of several alternative courses of action, you can be confident that you have *enough* information to make a good decision, a decision that has a reasonable expectation of a favorable outcome. Confidence, you will recall, is one of the cornerstones of success. In reality, it is one of the few assets we can always count on in a fight considering the chaotic nature of reality. Confidence gives you an advantage.

The best known and most frequently quoted excerpt from Chinese general Sun Tzu's *The Art of War* is: "[If you] know your enemy and [also] know yourself . . . you will not be defeated in a hundred battles." This chapter has to do with recognizing the type of situation you are in and with knowing your enemy. The next chapter, Avoiding Errors, will concern itself with how to know yourself. To structure the material related to situations, we will use the keyword N-O-T-E.

> ....
> **The keyword N-O-T-E stands for:**
> **N**ature of the Situation
> **O**utcomes
> **T**actics
> **E**volution
> ....

In other words, take *note* of the circumstances surrounding the events or contest at hand in order to increase your chances of winning. Taking *note* involves pre-constructing a mental checklist of questions or items for consideration when a situation arises that requires a decision.

The checklist, having been set up when there was no pressure to decide something, serves as a structure for an organized thought process, a help in times of stress. Few people take the time to prepare themselves for effective decision making. This kind of preparation gives you an advantage.

The checklist approach we are recommending here may seem a bit cumbersome. Decision-making methodology, however, is probably one of those choices that was made for you somewhere in your past. Someone or some event taught you how to react to the need to decide. We think you should specifically and objectively review your own criteria so you can decide how you want to behave. Think it through, at least one time anyway. Ask yourself: "How do I go about deciding what to do?" Then make your own choice.

The items on your checklist should be developed from your personal experience. There are simply too many possibilities for populating the list. As individuals differ from each other, so do their decision criteria. And, necessarily so! What works for one may be disaster for another. In each of the sections related to the discussion of N-O-T-E below, we are going to suggest a few ideas you might use as starting points. Expand these ideas and create your own checklist. Then, put it to work until it becomes habit.

N-O-T-E
NATURE OF THE SITUATION

You want to be able to conceptualize the nature of a situation or problem in an almost geometric fashion. Try to get a mental picture of the dimensions, a feel for the dynamics and forces that are interacting. Let's take a look at some questions you might ask.

♦ Is the decision unusual or routine? Routine decisions have established precedents which can be followed. For unusual decisions, more analysis and consideration may be required. The differences between routine and unusual decisions are not the same as the differences between critical and trivial decisions. For example, the decision to accelerate through a yellow traffic light may be routine, but it is not trivial, because the outcome, if unfavorable, may take your life.

♦ Is the cost of the decision high or low in monetary units? In "relationship" (love, friendship, trust) units? Can you afford the cost of a bad decision?

♦ Is the decision related strictly to business or is it strictly personal? Does the outcome of the decision overlap both areas?

♦ Are the effects of the decision long-term or short-term? In Chapter 7 we will consider the long-term impact of seemingly short-term decisions a little more closely.

OUTCOMES

Sun Tzu says, "Expect the worst." A popular saying goes, "Expect the best, but plan for the worst." We advise a middle-of-the-road approach. Forecast your outcomes based on likelihood of occurrence. Make at least three projections. Think through what can happen on the upside and then on the downside; last, forecast what you consider to be the more likely outcome (which should fall somewhere in the middle).

Make contingency plans for both high side and low side outcomes. However, plan in detail for the expected outcome. General Dwight Eisenhower said this about planning:

> The virtue of planning is not that your plans will work out, but that you will have thought through the various outcomes beforehand. That way, when things do not go according to plans (which almost always happens), you will have considered a number of scenarios ahead of time and will have a strong head start for making revisions.

In Hold 'em, it is an absolute necessity, in order to make appropriate bets, to project expected value of those bets. Projecting expected values requires a good understanding of pot odds (both actual and implied) along with the ability to accurately count outs. Betting when the pot odds are positive and folding when they are negative is fundamental to winning. As Sun Tzu advises, "Advance when you can win, retreat when you cannot." We will provide a great deal more detail about betting strategy in later chapters of the book.

TACTICS

Development of winning tactics is an art. There are an infinite number of tactical subelements that can be combined to build major tactical variations. Two overriding questions need to be answered in the process of building tactics.

1. Can the proposed tactics achieve the desired outcome?

2. Can the proposed tactics be accomplished using resources (manpower, money, and material) that are available?

Developing tactics requires a trip into the land of "what-if"—a place populated with tremendous amounts of uncertainty, multiple types of ambiguity, and a host of differing viewpoints. It is easy to see the need for a development process that is strictly joined to the co-requirements of utility and accomplishment.

In the land of imagination, fear and greed cast very long shadows. Managing the effects of phantom fears and gargantuan greediness requires discipline (which is acquired through training and practice) and knowledge (which is acquired through study and practice). The material contained in this book is specifically designed to help you get ready for challenges before they occur. It is too late to prepare when opportunity or threat is knocking on your door.

EVOLUTION

The last term in the keyword N-O-T-E is evolution. We use this term in a military sense. That is, *evolution* is the manner in which the situation progresses or evolves as both tactic and counter-tactic dynamically interact across time. However well constructed, tactics and strategies that do not consider, at the very least, those scenarios that are more likely to emerge from the current one are fundamentally flawed. It's a "win-the-battle, lose-the-war" syndrome.

Playing tournament Hold 'em successfully requires keeping a careful eye on the leader board. Your position on the board, particularly as players get nearer to the money, should certainly have an impact on your willingness to enter into certain pots. If you have few chips, but might just limp into the money, you may avoid playing any but the most powerful starting hands. If you have few chips and feel you cannot make the money without doubling up, you might take more chances.

Deciding to Compete

When you are faced with circumstances that require you to contend with other people or organizations, your decisions about how and when to compete should be based on solid reasoning. Of course, competition may be suddenly forced on you by external factors, but in many, if not most, competitive situations (especially in Hold 'em, where you always have time, and should always take time, to think through your actions), you will have an opportunity to consider your approach. We suggest that you use the keyword R-A-P-T to examine competitive prospects prior to entering the contest.

....

The four critical areas represented by the keyword R-A-P-T are:

Readiness

Alternatives

Point of Attack

Timing

....

R-A-P-T

READINESS

Examine your level of *Readiness* to determine your relative ability to sustain the effort involved in the competition you face. Elements of readiness might include physical readiness, financial readiness, technical readiness, educational readiness, and readiness of spirit.

Many people have the goal of becoming professional poker players. Texas Hold 'em is an extremely trying way to earn a living. There is no way you can avoid tripping over your own weaknesses. Like it or not (mostly not), you will make mistakes that cost you money and that are simply embarrassing because you will know better.

Hold 'em really tests the spirit. You might spend years of practice to develop your skills to a level you believe is fairly high, only to find you are not able to play up to that level in real competition. Failure is discouraging and hard to rationalize. Look within yourself before setting out to conquer the poker world. Make sure you can handle the pain, because success is not guaranteed, nor is it common.

ALTERNATIVES

Consider *alternative* paths for approaching the competition in light of your estimates of readiness. Some paths will be smoother than others because you have some kind of advantage. Further, considering alternatives often illuminates opportunities that may have been over-looked if you rush to respond to a challenge.

Hold 'em offers a wide variety of choices for playing structure. The choices you make relative to your temperament and skill level will determine whether you are able to profit from the game. For example, the choice of Limit versus No Limit Hold 'em is not trivial. The strategies applied in each type of structure are definitely and critically different. Further, the level of competition you face will vary widely. Players who are sitting at a $2/$4 Limit table will be quite different from those at a $2/$5 No Limit table. Before you jump into a game, consider where you might fit given your level of experience and your appetite for risk.

POINT OF ATTACK

The *point of attack* can be thought of as the place where you want to apply the power and momentum of your competitive initiative, the tip of the spear. You should carefully weigh two factors of the competitive situation in determining the point of attack. First, evaluate the relative strength of the opponent's defensive measures at the point of attack. Sun Tzu says, "Attack weakness with strength." Select a point of attack that allows you to leverage any advantage you might have against a corresponding flaw or crack in the defense.

Second, assess the relative value of likely points of attack in the equation of victory. There may be several possible avenues of approach to your opponent, but only one or two that lead to targets that, if defeated or captured, have any real importance in determining which side wins the contest.

When playing No Limit Hold 'em, you may face the choice of whether to attempt to win a number of smaller pots or focus on winning one or two big ones. We realize that doing both at the same time is preferable, but it is often incompatible because of the relative tightness/looseness of other players. Tight opponents will allow more, but smaller, pots. Loose opponents, fewer, but larger pots. You will be required to evaluate the makeup of the table you face and determine which approach might offer the highest return. Your approach to your opponents will therefore affect how many hands you play and the level of aggressiveness you display when you bet.

TIMING

No matter how well conceived, actions will fail if they are not timed appropriately. Timing is the one overarching critical variable in determining the success of competitive actions. Effective timing is supported by two factors. First, effective timing is developed through experience and knowledge gained from realistic practice. Nothing takes the place of the "feel of rightness" acquired from doing something over and over until it becomes intuitive. Second, effective timing is based on accurate assessment of up-to-date information. Information is the key to timing. If you know what your opponents are planning, you can time your actions to defeat them.

Timing determines the success of many plays in Hold 'em. For example, stealing blinds is a matter of timing. Effective semi-bluffing is also a function of timing. Underlying both of these plays is a sense of what your opponent is doing. In order to time your plays well, pay attention to your opponent. You may not be able to read his mind all the time, but your opponent will often reveal his thoughts in unexpected ways.

It is probably *not* good to focus your attention on the common *tells* you might read about. Focusing on tells tends to encourage you to see what you are looking for and to not see other indicators which may be more important. Just relax and observe your opponents. Try not to judge anything about their appearance or manner (although, it is very difficult not to make those judgments). Instead, watch objectively. People give themselves away through small actions and expressions. If you keep an open, observant eye on them, you might just pick up the signal.

 "Tells" are detectable aspects of behavior that can, if properly analyzed, indicate the nature and strength of other players' holdings.

Applying patterned logic to competitive situations assures you will think through all the relevant issues before embarking on a course of action. The most common mistake we make in playing a hand of poker is moving too quickly based on incomplete analysis of the situation. When the play is over, and usually after we have lost a few bucks, we can look back and see that if we had just taken a moment to figure out what options we had, we probably would have acted in another way. Practice logical patterns of working your way through decisions and you will make better and more profitable choices.

7

Avoiding Errors

FOR THE PURPOSES of discussion in this chapter, we begin by defining the word "failure." A *failure* is any decision process or set of actions that leads to an outcome that does not, in full or in part, realize one's desired objective. A failure is also an "error" (or "mistake") when the decision process used or the set of actions undertaken is based on faulty reasoning, poor planning, disregard of facts, misunderstanding or miscommunication among participants, emotional reactions, lack of due diligence, or any of a multitude of similar indicators of preventable ignorance and underperformance. In short, *failure* occurs when you do not achieve your objectives; failure becomes *error* when said lack of achievement could have been prevented by reasonable means.

It is particularly important to distinguish between *failure* and *error* in playing Texas Hold 'em. It is entirely likely that a player may fail to win a given tournament or a given pot while at the same time making no errors, perhaps even playing brilliantly. Perfect play, even brilliant play, carries with it no guarantee of success because the fall of the cards (that is, the point of collision between probability and reality) is the critical factor in determining outcomes.

The same, unfortunately, is true in business situations and careers. Good fortune easily triumphs over common sense, mental acuity, and even education. This is the reason that patience and control of emotion are the more obvious marks of a real champion. The only thing you can realistically expect to accomplish in life is to put yourself in a position to win.

The Six Causes of Failure

In *The Art of War,* Sun Tzu lists six major causes of failure. (As an aside, we refer often to Sun Tzu because his short masterpiece, despite its rather bellicose title, is a book about human nature. Human nature, and the manipulation thereof, has not changed in the 2,500 years since the time of Sun Tzu. The principles cited in *The Art of War* are the starting points for success in any and every competitive situation.) The six causes of failure are:

1. Lack of resources (a shortage of cash, chips, manpower, technology, equipment, or mental acuity)

2. Lack of direction (failure to specify or adhere to objectives)

3. Lack of performance (inability or unwillingness to complete necessary tasks)

4. Lack of discipline (loss of emotional control)

5. Lack of order (disorganized thinking and reasoning)

6. Lack of competence (deficiencies in experience or knowledge)

After reviewing this list, we would have to admit that it is virtually impossible to enter into every contest with each one of the six causes of failure completely covered. Most of the time, you will need to manage weakness in one area or another. The fact that weakness exists, however, is not a reason to ignore that weakness or to gloss it over. If you are aware of a weakness (and you should be), you have the opportunity to take reasonable steps to compensate for it. Weakness can be turned to strength by careful planning and effective execution of plans.

Encouraging Errors in Others

Every time one of your opponents or competitors commits an error, you have an opportunity to gain an advantage. The more often others can be encouraged to trip and fall, the more often you will win. Therefore, understanding how to promote the other fellow's mistakes is an important skill. The best way to push other players and competitors into making mistakes is by creating or magnifying some type of strong emotional reaction (negative or positive) that disrupts their good judgment and interferes with effective decision processes. The types of emotion you want to amplify are fear, greed, anger, lust, arrogance, insecurity, etc.

The idea is to aid your opponents in throwing away their emotional control; to assist them with any tendency they might have to *discard* their better judgment. To help you remember a few of the many approaches to creating emotional agitation in others, we use the keyword D-I-S-C-A-R-D.

··
The actions represented by the keyword D-I-S-C-A-R-D are:
Defend
Inflate
Scare
Crowd
Antagonize
Reduce
Distract
··

Before we continue, you may be interested in hearing how this particularly acerbic keyword came into existence. One of our co-authors, Don Krause, played in the 2006 World Series of Poker

(WSOP). During the WSOP, Don also participated in quite a few $2/$5 No Limit cash games at various casinos on the strip (for research purposes only, of course). During one of these $2/$5 sessions, in the wee hours of the morning, he had the opportunity to play with a number of (mostly) young men and women who made at least a portion of their income hustling tourists at the poker table. Once they found out Don was writing a book on poker, some of these folks had no reservations about discussing their trade secrets. The keyword D-I-S-C-A-R-D is based on these discussions. Hence, the following material might be subtitled, "A Vegas Hustler's Guide to Landing a Fish!"

DEFEND

The idea behind the word *defend* is to lower the other person's natural barriers by befriending, defending, and supporting him at the table. It is not uncommon for a bad player to get lucky and win a hand he should surely have lost. It is further not uncommon for the losing player, in these situations, to verbally ostracize the winning player. By defending the winner, you may attract some unwelcome verbal barbs. But as the hero coming to his defense (virtually everyone at the poker table secretly believes *he* really does deserve to win, despite poor play), you may lower the level of suspicion about your motives for being pleasant. Further, by sympathizing and empathizing with his (albeit faulty) reasoning when he loses a hand, you may be able to keep him at the table a little longer.

INFLATE

The word *inflate* implies boosting another player's ego. This method is a special favorite of the attractive young ladies at the table. It succeeds particularly well with men, for some reason. Here is how it is done. The young lady sits down at the table, fumbles around for a few hands, then smilingly asks one of the guys for help in understanding how to play her cards, which he is more than happy to provide. She then, smilingly, helps herself to his chips a few hands later.

If, by the way, you are chuckling right now and thinking that such a corny vaudeville skit would never really happen, think again. Some guys can be extremely gullible after downing a few drinks. Pots in a decent $2/$5 No Limit game in a Vegas casino can easily reach more than $300. All a person need do is win one or two good-size pots a night to clear a nice profit. Win a few pots, then leave. Easy money.

SCARE

To *scare* or intimidate other players requires taking a bit of a risk. First, you must get a good hand or be able to represent a good hand. This requires patience. Second, you must be willing to bet heavily. This requires courage. If you are able to scatter the table a few times, most players will become wary and tend to back off when you bet. Ideally, you can then isolate a conservative, somewhat tentative, player and push him out of one or two fairly large pots.

CROWD

Crowding is a form of physical intimidation. Card tables used for Texas Hold 'em comfortably seat eight or nine players. Most casinos seat ten players at a table. Ten players at a table invites crowding. By invading another person's private space even a little bit, you can make them uncomfortable and nervous.

ANTAGONIZE

The best way to *antagonize* another player is to deliver an expensive beat. The easiest players to antagonize are those that appear the most obviously arrogant at the table. Since arrogance is often used to veil nervousness or other weakness, delivering an expensive beat publicly embarrasses the person and exposes his weakness to ridicule. Arrogance and embarrassment do not mesh well.

REDUCE

To *reduce* means to make a person feel small. Reducing is done with criticism. People seem to be overly protective of their poker playing skills. Even a little criticism of their play will send some people into orbit.

DISTRACT

Distracting and annoying other players can be very effective and entails fairly low risk. You will need to be observant in order to pinpoint what creates the kind of response you want. Certain behaviors, language, dress, and food can be sources of annoyance for other people at the table. Further, a little bit of annoyance dispensed over an extended period of time can result in major emotional disruption and accompanying loss of judgment for a hand or two. Remember, it just takes a few hands a night to make the difference.

We have deliberately restricted our comments about the word D-I-S-C-A-R-D to situations encountered at the poker table. Extending these ideas into the workplace or marketplace is a minor jump of imagination. Anything that is effective at the poker table will be just as effective in other venues.

Keep in mind, however, that your relationships at the poker table tend to be short and easily terminated. Relationships in other areas of life can be prolonged and the stakes involved can be quite high. Using any of the above tactics carelessly may result in more problems than profit in the long run. Proceed with caution.

Protecting Yourself from Errors

If encouraging errors by other people is one side of a winning coin, then preventing errors by you is the other side. The errors you make can and will be used against you if you find yourself competing in situations where real money or real power are at stake. Even in something as trivial (from the world's point of view) as a divorce proceeding can result in your opponent's learning more about your weaknesses and frailties than you would care to have them know.

Consider everything you contemplate doing from the position of a future employer, a future stockholder, a future loan officer, a future Senate confirmation hearing chairperson, a future political campaign opponent, or a future spouse's divorce attorney (to mention just a few). How are these people going to feel when (not if) they find out about what you just did? How can they use it against you (and they will)? The best defense against errors and the damage they will bestow upon your reputation is to W-A-L-K T-H-E L-I-N-E.

The eleven activities represented in W-A-L-K T-H-E
L-I-N-E are:

Watch Your Step

Anticipate Difficulty

Love Your Neighbor

Kneel to Power

Think Success

Hold Up Your End

Enter the Arena

Live Like Someone Is Watching

Imitate the Best

Nose to the Ground

Exit on Cue

WATCH YOUR STEP

There are plenty of potholes along the path of success. If you insist on keeping your head in the clouds, you will end up with your face in the dirt. Strike a working balance between sparkling optimism and gritty pessimism. Keep your eyes on the path as you stride into the future.

ANTICIPATE DIFFICULTY

Difficulty lies hidden everywhere. Look for it. Learn to love difficulty and welcome the opportunity it almost always provides. It is not the fastest nor the best-dressed cowboy who shoots the straightest in a fight; it is the one whose hand does not tremble when bullets are flying in his direction. Train yourself to thrive and perform under circumstances that others find uncomfortable or frightening.

LOVE YOUR NEIGHBOR

Love your neighbor? After all we have said so far, what is this advice? Simple, you can climb the heights of success in one of two ways. First way: stack up the bodies of the opponents you have defeated and clamber up the pile. Or, second way: stand on the shoulders of those who want to help you succeed. Guess which is easier and more effective?

This bit of advice in no way, however, implies that you must be a fool in regard to your neighbors. If they insist on dying or losing their shirt to help you get ahead, well, let them (or oblige them, as the case may be.) Keep in mind that it is not those neighbors whose bodies are lying prostrate on the battlefields of career or commerce who can help you get ahead. It is far more profitable to love the ones who are still standing.

KNEEL TO POWER

There will always be something you need or want. As a result, so far as your need or want extends beyond your personal capacity to provide, there will always be some individuals who have power over you. Kneeling to power to get what you want is preferable to stealing from power. It certainly creates less resentment and difficulty in the long run.

THINK SUCCESS

A little positive visualization goes a long way. See yourself gaining your objectives. Maintain that vision in your mind's eye, clearly and constantly. Combine a spoonful of visualization with a gallon or two of hard-nosed determination and you have the formula for achievement.

HOLD UP YOUR END

Not many people keep weasels as pets. If you make a deal, hold up your end of it, particularly when it becomes inconvenient or expensive. Following this advice requires refraining from entering into commitments you cannot uphold. Reputation clings like crazy glue. It stays right there, no matter how hard you scrub. Further, when your reputation stinks, the only people who will stick with you are the skunks.

Under practical circumstances, it is almost impossible to honor to the letter every bargain you make. Things and conditions change over time, often in unpredictable and unfortunate ways. At the time you enter into long-term commitments, consider the wisdom of an escape clause. It is often too late to negotiate parole after the crime has been committed and the cell door is locked.

ENTER THE ARENA

We have made this point before and will make it again. You cannot enjoy the benefits of success while standing on the sidelines. You must play the game and you must win in order to achieve your goals. Sometimes the game you play is not the one you would have chosen under other circumstances, but that is no excuse for failing yourself. Get in there. Half of winning is suiting up for the game. (It's half of losing, too, but you have no choice anyway, at least not if you intend to live your life and not just exist for a few meaningless years.)

LIVE LIKE SOMEONE IS WATCHING

There is no part of your life, perhaps other than your own thoughts (and that is not for sure) that cannot be monitored intentionally by anyone with enough resources. Moreover, a great deal of what we do each day is unintentionally monitored. A person cannot move in the normal course of business without being photographed some-where—the bank, the mall, the gas station, the ATM. The ubiquitous cell phone is the equivalent of an electronic monitoring device. For your own protection, you must live your life as if someone is observing what you do at all times (yes, ALL times.) For all you really know, they are. Get over it. Use it to your advantage. (Everything has an upside. Don't be a fool and waste it.)

IMITATE THE BEST

Studying other people and selecting the best as role models is an effective method of self-improvement. The only danger is extending the role-model's special talent or expertise into other areas. Good ball players are good ball players. Most of the time, they are nothing more. Politicians are politicians. Musicians are musicians. Be sure to differentiate among attributes before adopting a set of them without reserve.

NOSE TO THE GROUND

Opportunity doesn't usually knock. A good deal of the time it just farts softly and the only thing you notice is a slight odor. Even more often, the chance to gain an advantage comes disguised as hard work. This is so true that anything that looks like opportunity, but does not require a lot of effort should be viewed with suspicion. Be assured, if you search for it diligently, opportunity will sooner or later show up. But it will almost never be dressed like you thought it would be or smell like success at the beginning. Prepare thoroughly, wait patiently, watch sharply, jump quickly.

EXIT ON CUE

Success comes in waves. There are peaks and valleys. When you have had a run and life sends you a cue that it is time to take your bow and get off the stage, do so. Another mark of a champion is knowing when to leave the party. Overstaying your welcome almost always carries serious consequences. Learn to recognize the signs.

8

Requirements, Risk, and Reward

IN CHAPTERS 3 to 7 we discussed ideas related to Confidence, Anger, Frustration, Fear, Luck, Logic, and Errors—all in the context of developing the character needed to face the challenge of winning at Texas Hold 'em and nurturing success in your career and other competitive aspects of business and personal life. In this chapter, we will be concerned with aspects of the Requirements, and Risks versus Rewards. Specifically, we will pose two critical questions for you to think about. First, where can you begin? Second, what is at stake? Further, since we cannot (and would not presume to) answer the questions for you, we will advance some concepts which may help you frame appropriate answers for your personal situation.

Requirements

First question: Where can you begin? Implementing many, if not most, of the suggestions we have made so far will require some level of change on your part. Change, even small change, can be difficult to face and complicated to put into practice. In order to produce a change in your life, you must be convinced—at your basic emotional level, not just intellectually—that the change will somehow create a benefit for you.

A basic law of human behavior is that people act according to what they *believe* is in their best interest. (Of course, understanding this law is essential to reading other people's real intentions and, in Hold 'em, reading the hands they are or are not holding.)

We introduced the following ideas (highly summarized here) over the first five chapters of Part One:

♦ Confidence is derived from deciding for ourselves where we intend to direct our lives. Confidence bestows the power to act.

♦ Character flaws can be quite detrimental to achieving goals. Anger, frustration, and fear are natural components of the competitive environment, but they can be attenuated and must be managed.

♦ The effects of luck on the outcome of events and decisions, however, cannot be attenuated, managed, or even avoided. We must live with our luck, good or bad. It does not help to go on tilt over outcomes that are out of our control once the cards are dealt.

♦ Applying appropriate logic to analyzing decision alternatives improves the quality of decisions (and possibly, some believe anyhow, enhances the luck component of outcomes. In other words, the harder you work, the luckier you—might—get. Even if you do not get luckier, however, hard work seems to pay off in many respects, including increasing your self-esteem).

♦ Some level of failure to achieve objectives can be expected in almost every activity, but errors and mistakes in thinking and planning allow others to win easily. Defend your future by maintaining vigilance and discipline.

That brings us back to the first question: Where can you begin? The answer is straightforward. You can begin by deciding to act on your desires. The nature, the shape, and the context of your desires, those things you want out of your life, even if they are a bit fuzzy, even if you do not have a magnificent obsession (but, surely you want something) provide a marker, a signpost, pointing in a direction you can move. Your ideas may (and probably will) evolve as you move forward, but your desires right now are a good place to start. If you frequently think about making a certain journey, accomplishing a certain objective, doing a certain task, achieving a certain milestone, then that is the direction to go.

D-I-C-E

So, how do you actually take the first step, given that all current indicators (or people) in your life may be pointing or pulling you somewhere else? We suggest a technique represented by the keyword D-I-C-E.

··

The keyword D-I-C-E stands for:

D (Desire, Decide, Detail)

I (Invest, Intensify)

C (Conform, Collect, Construct)

E Effectuate

··

We consider this technique to be extremely reliable, since it is based on principles and instructions that are as old as human civilization. Some of the earliest philosophical writings known contain this particular method for getting results. Everyone, and we do mean everyone, who accomplishes anything in life *on purpose* uses some variation of this method. D-I-C-E is a very powerful tool, which is easy to learn and absolutely will not fail if you simply apply it to your situation.

DESIRE, DECIDE, DETAIL

It seems you cannot get away from making a decision about what you *desire*. Many people fear making such a decision because it seems to place them on the path toward the unknown. We are not going to tell you to be unconcerned about decisions. On the contrary, think hard about what you want. But beyond creating the motivation to use rational caution, fear of the unknown is useless. Any and all decisions (even NO decisions) point you toward the unknown. There are no safe havens. Even pocket aces get cracked a bit too often it seems. Some unknowns may be better than others, but it is hard to tell which ones from where you are standing right now, that is, in the present moment, before you make a decision.

Therefore, make the best choice you can with available information. *Decide* which set of your desires you wish to pursue. Then describe that set in *detail*. Daydream about it. See the fulfillment of your desire in your mind's eye as often as possible. There is no need to push or try to force anything to happen. Pushing will definitely not help you get where you are intending to go. Relax. Take it easy. Roll along your path from moment to moment, day to day, keeping your desire in front of you in as much detail as possible, taking whatever action may be appropriate.

(If this type of activity seems a lot like what you do anyway, you are probably close to correct. The critical difference lies in deciding and detailing. Most of the time we are quite undetermined about what we want to do, and our goals are quite vague. We tend to vacillate, allowing our minds to jump around among the many, sometimes conflicting, desires we encounter on a daily basis. This process leads nowhere in particular, much less any place we might actually *want* to go.)

Clarity will take about a week of regular practice. Ten minutes a day will do the trick: ten minutes a day of uninterrupted, relaxed daydreaming about the goals and desires you have decided to pursue. It's very easy. Do not push. Just relax. Dream, but dream clearly and vividly.

INVEST, INTENSIFY

Emotions fuel dreams. Emotions fire imagination. Emotions encourage heart. In order to move along the path of your desires, you must invest your emotions into your decision. Your desires must burn with an intensity that you can feel. Investing intense emotion into your desires is the critical point for success. Emotional intensity is the catalyst for turning wishful thinking into real accomplishment.

Emotional intensity can exist only if your decision actually means something to you, only if it leads in the direction of your preferred, selected vision of the future. But what if the vision of the future you have selected collides sharply with reality? What if you simply cannot get there from here, today. Worse, what if you are thrown into the path of some ugly unforeseen event or some nasty individual that fouls up your plans.

Two facts of life:

Most people make more than one intermediate stop along the path before achieving their goals.

The dreams you dream at one place and time may (and probably should) differ markedly from those you will dream in another place and time.

You will, more than once in your life, say thanks that you did not achieve your earlier goals. You will also, more than once, find yourself shedding bitter tears when you do reach some cherished goal that quickly turns to dust in your hands.

Reality is contrary and perverse. (Or, as one of our grandmothers used to quip, "Ain't life grand!") Great poker players are long-term idealists and short-term realists. It would be nice to eventually win the tournament, but the next hand is the important one because the next hand is the one that might knock you out if you are not paying attention. Understand where you are trying go, but keep your eyes on the road signs in case a detour becomes necessary.

CONFORM, COLLECT, CONSTRUCT

The key to greatness—that is, the key to maintaining durable idealism and continuing emotional intensity in the face of immediate reality's tendency to serve up choking frustration and frequent failure—is to utilize the people, events, and objects revealed by the chaos of the moment to assist you in moving onward. Any other approach contributes to your becoming bogged down where you are and eventually losing sight of your target and losing the motivation to reach it.

The idea here is represented by the words conform, collect, and construct. To *conform* to reality means that you make an effort to see and evaluate the situations you encounter for what they are. Objectivity in dealing with people and challenges is a critical virtue because objectivity smoothes out the highs and lows. Generally speaking, you will make better judgments when you look for the hidden value in unfavorable events and the hidden threat in favorable ones.

Objectivity in evaluating situations in Hold 'em is fundamental. If you see only the cards you want to see, you will seldom last very long at the table. Conforming implies, however, neither agreement nor acquiescence. It simply suggests using the art of seeing clearly to the best of your ability.

Removing emotional bias from your evaluations of people and events as much as possible allows you to more readily *collect* available assets. Each incident you experience presents its own unique opportunities. Collecting information and resources from these "real" opportunities supplies the resources you need to move toward your own defined goals.

Watching how other people play hands when you are sitting out really helps. Things seldom work out as anticipated. People who become bogged down in regret, blame, or retribution miss the chance to use what has actually occurred to their advantage. Sort out the pieces left over after reality happens. Pick up those that are useful. *Construct* the tools and relationships required to craft your own path.

EFFECTUATE

Effectuate means to make or cause something to happen. Take a step. Move away from the spot where you are standing. There has got to be some small step you can take in the direction of your desires. Take that step today. If you make progress toward your goals each day, you will eventually reach them.

"Easier said than done!" you reply. No time. No money. Too much responsibility. I have kids. Pets. Cars. Debts. Whatever. Is it that you are expecting there will be a time when these concerns do not exist, a magic moment when they can be set aside and you can move freely? The only magic moment you will ever get is right now. If you do not make it happen now, then when?

There is some part of what you want, however small or trivial, that you can get now. Throw the D-I-C-E. Reach for it. Take it. Savor the rush. You brought something you want into your life. You will enjoy the feeling.

Risk and Reward

Evaluating the risk and reward involved when you bet in Hold 'em is a fundamental and critical factor in winning. So the second question we ask is: If you begin a journey toward your ideals and goals, what can you possibly gain? If you risk going all-in in Hold 'em, you gain the pot if you win. In other aspects of competition, it may not be as clear. But no matter what you accomplish, whether you win or lose in monetary value, the self-respect and peace of mind that accompany pursuing your own goals are, in fact, priceless.

From a practical point of view, since cost or investment very nearly always come before reward, we strongly advocate balancing the cost of actions against the expected value of likely results. In Hold 'em, this kind of calculation is possible (if barely), but not very precise because of the many assumptions being made. In interpersonal competitive decisions, risk and reward are much harder to assess. But risk cannot be avoided, and reward is somewhat arbitrary, even if you make the correct moves every time.

A-N-T-E Up

Whenever you become involved in an effort to better yourself through seeking some kind of reward, you will face opposition, obstacles, and challenges. These competitive factors will force you to ante up something before you can play the game: money, time, relationship value, something. Every time you are required to ANTE up, think through these four issues associated with the word A-N-T-E, and, correspondingly, how much it may really cost to enter the game.

....

The four issues associated with the word A-N-T-E are:
  Anticipate Risk
  Numbers Rule
  Target Gains and Losses
  Expect Deceit

....

ANTICIPATE RISK

There is no such thing as a risk-free decision. Every choice you make entails more or less risk, much of which is not identifiable nor even tangible. Accepting the risks inherent in poker means, most prominently and explicitly, that you must be willing to go all-in with a reasonable chance to win, but not necessarily holding the nuts. If you are not able to accept this level of risk in Hold 'em at appropriate times, you cannot win at Poker in the long-run.

Similar situations present themselves in the interpersonal arena. At some time during your life, you will be required to bet on one or more situations that have significant inherent risk. If you cannot go for it when necessary and appropriate, higher levels of achievement or wealth may not be available to you (except by the operation of chance). But even if you are inclined to risk little and, accordingly, you expect little, in pursuit of your goals, you need to anticipate some level of risk. With risk comes loss; be prepared for it all the time.

NUMBERS RULE

Do the math whenever you can. It is not necessary to be a math wiz to understand uncomplicated profit and loss figures. If you are willing to probe at the context and details of a situation for some type of measurable variables (e.g., dollars involved, interest rate, expected return, total investment, expected sales, how much is in it for me?, how much do you get?, etc), and then analyze them, even if superficially, you will often quickly uncover the weak spots in otherwise good looking investments or bets.

Understand poker math enough to compute pot odds (a lot more on this later in Chapter 13.) Understand home loans, IRA investments, higher education borrowing, and other normal, but significant, financial aspects of adult life in the twenty-first century well enough to have some chance to recognize a bad beat before it is laid upon you. If you have good numbers and analyze them adequately, they will present useful aspects of the situation. Not all aspects, maybe, but pay attention to those you can measure.

TARGET GAINS AND LOSSES

One of the more problematic rules of "good gambling" (or risk-taking) is to set your limits. Quit while you are ahead; stop when you have lost what you can afford to lose. The rule is, granted, nearly impossible to follow in the heat of the moment. Despite this, it is a great idea to target gains and losses and keep some type of record, if for no other reason than to know what you started with and where you ended up, for sure.

EXPECT DECEIT

Unfortunately, human nature being what it is, you must expect that others are currently deceiving you or will deceive you in the future, particularly in deals where money, power, or status is at stake. No one is immune from deceit. The closer a person is to you, and the more implicit trust you place in that person, the greater opportunity that person has to deceive you.

When you sit down to play, take a hard look around the table. Everyone there, regardless of previous or current relationships, is susceptible to the power of human emotions—most particularly, greed, envy, fear, anger, and lust—and the deceit that inevitably follows them. Be wary, be flexible, be prepared. Success or failure often depend on whether you maintain your poise and confidence in the face of what may seem to you to be devastating betrayal of confidence.

PART TWO

OPPORTUNITY

Chinese general Sun Tzu made an astute observation about the nature of opportunity: "The opportunity to lose is created by one's own decisions; the opportunity to win by decisions of one's opponent." In other words, using our own resources, we can develop a good defense, one that will prevent us from losing the battle. In order to win, however, our opponent must create an opportunity for us. Winning is always a function of finding and using our opponent's tendencies against him. The side that gives up the least information and makes the fewest mistakes wins the battle.

9

The Land of Oz

Classifying Players

IN HOLD 'EM, you will often hear comments about "playing the cards" or "playing the person." When we "play the cards" we are essentially employing a defensive strategy. By almost always opening up with premium starting hands, we are putting ourselves in a good defensive position, a position from which we will win or lose only a little, most of the time. Certainly, the best cards before the flop will often win the pot. Hence, we stand a better chance of coming out on top when we are playing good hands to start with.

But despite placing yourself in a fairly strong position from the point of view of opening card values, when you use a premium opening hand strategy, it becomes easy for other players to read you. A tight player may bet or call only about one out of every five hands. When he does bet, and especially if he bets aggressively, everyone at the table knows that he has a decent starting hand. This knowledge tends to reduce the number of individuals who are willing to call those bets, limiting pot size and reducing potential profit from winning hands.

Most professional Hold 'em players recommend "playing the player," rather than strictly "playing the cards." This means, at a minimum, that you take every chance you get to assess other players at the table in order to determine strengths and weaknesses. "Playing the player" is an aggressive strategy. Its success depends on how well you are able to "read" the other players in terms of their attributes and tendencies that affect their preference of hands to play and their manner of betting those hands.

When you "play the player," your choice of starting hands will be determined by a mix of factors related to information provided by other players. For instance, your position in the order of betting relative to players whom you perceive as weaker or stronger than you should significantly influence your choice of hands to enter a pot.

Over the course of the next couple of chapters, we will provide you with criteria for assessing other players' tendencies and making those tendencies work against them. We will also provide some evaluative methods for assessing strength of opening hands and guidelines for pre-flop betting. A critical law of competition is that no strategy works all the time. *Every* tactic has a counter-tactic that *will* defeat it. The best players in the world can be taken down if you understand their method of play and discover where it is weak.

This idea is at the very core of Sun Tzu's comment above. If you win a contest, it is because your opponent gives you the opportunity. He will not, however, provide that opportunity intentionally. He will provide it because you have studied his methods and manner. He will provide it because you can anticipate his card choices and betting strategies under different circumstances. He will provide it by doing things which telegraph his intentions and actions (i.e., tells).

The Quantum Mechanics of Behavior

Imagine for a moment that human personality and associated behavior patterns, like the human body and other types of matter in the universe, are comprised of quantum particles. For purposes of discussion, we will call these particles "behavioral nodes." Like their subatomic cousins—electrons, quarks, leptons, photons, gluons, bosons, and gravitons—behavioral nodes spin (for illustration purposes, either right or left) around an axis, or center line. The axis consists of two extreme behavior points (i.e., polar points), such as, in Hold 'em, "sloppy loose" (plays 100 percent of hands except when in the restroom) at one pole, or "super-glue tight" (plays only AA, KK, QQ, AK) at the other pole. The center line axis drawn between the two polar extremes represents all the intermediate levels of tight/loose play. The exact behavior of an individual at any given time is a function of where his preference point on the axis lies, and what type of spin and tilt are being applied to him by internal and external forces at the moment of decision.

You can observe the spin property in operation by watching the interaction among participants of a group discussion, particularly where there is a difference of opinion among them. The tone, content, and body language associated with each participant's comments will contain elements of spin that reflect the combined bias of the speaker's underlying behavioral node configurations with respect to the topic under discussion and/or whatever subcontextual issues are involved. (For example, subcontext happens when a participant wants to impress one or more members of the group with his knowledge of a subject under discussion, even when he has no real interest in it. No matter what he says, the subcontext is the message. Reading subcontext is the essence of reading tells at the poker table.)

Carrying this idea over into the realm of Hold 'em, the idea behind identifying individual behavioral characteristics and behavioral nodes is to grab the opportunity to "tilt" the opponent on one or more behavioral axes every chance you are given. This will cause the person to lose focus on the game, at least momentarily, while he readjusts his internal balance. Loss of focus by your opponent, even for a short period of time, gives you an immediate advantage. And gaining enough advantage means achieving victory.

Most poker books classify players using two simple behavioral nodes. First, players are classified on an axis ranging from loose (plays larger number of hands) to tight (plays fewer hands). Second, players are classified on an axis ranging from aggressive (bets and raises hands more frequently) to passive (calls, checks, and folds hands more frequently). Most poker books suggest that a tight, aggressive player is the model to emulate and a loose, passive player is the model to avoid.

Human personalities, however, tend to exhibit a far greater array of dimensions than those suggested by the two above. The greater the number of dimensions you can associate with an individual, the more chances you will gain to tilt him. Under the pressure of competition, particularly when results achieved are not those desired and frustration sets in, people begin to exhibit a mix of actions that, under calmer circumstances, they would keep under wraps. These actions signal where the behavioral fault lines are located. Using appropriate leverage, the fault lines can be exploited causing a tilt in perspective and judgment.

Understanding the nature and implications of various behaviors exhibited under stress will provide you with a point of departure for classifying people into competitive profiles and assessing weakness and strength. The key to the process for eliciting unguarded behaviors is inducing or reinforcing stress, which is a major factor in causing behavioral nodes to tilt on their axes. A normal person (that is, someone who is not a trained actor or skilled con artist) will be less capable of masking his real behaviors and intentions under stress, and therefore much more likely to make judgmental errors.

A word of caution, however. Behavioral stereotyping on the level suggested in this chapter is truly just a starting point, a way of structuring your thinking about understanding other people. The idea is to take your initial impressions of a person's behavior and tentatively fit them into a model like the one shown in Figure 9–1.

After comparing behaviors predicted by the model to behaviors actually observed over a period of time, you can determine which parts of the model more closely fit the person and which could be used to make predictions about that person's future behaviors.

You will, more often than not, be required to revise your initial conclusions as you gain more experience playing or interacting with a certain individual. Do not bet everything on first impressions (because you may be dealing with a person who is an expert at using

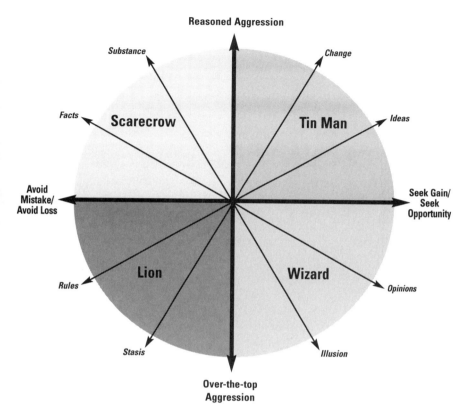

FIGURE 9–1

intentional deception, like a trained actor or con artist, particularly at the poker table or in critical interpersonal competitive situations). Be willing to revise your estimates. In other words, use the M-A-S-T process to firm up your estimates.

The keyword **M-A-S-T** stands for:

Measure

Analyze

Synthesize

Test

The OZ-Type Behavior Matrix

Figure 9–1 provides a straightforward behavioral matrix based on characters from the Wizard of Oz. Because the Land of Oz and its major characters are firmly rooted in our collective consciousness from childhood, we are able to use aspects of these characters to create a solid and memorable association with selected behavioral traits.

Please note once again that there is nothing particularly scientific about the traits and aspects shown on the matrix. They are simply descriptive and were developed specifically to assist readers of this book understand the evaluative processes suggested here.

Many authors of pop management books (such as this one) over the last three or four decades have postulated similar matrices to describe behavioral traits. The most valuable feature of the matrices seems to be creating an organized visual object which captures the highlights of what would otherwise be an esoteric (read "boring") philosophical discussion about concepts of human behavior. Since "a picture is worth a thousand words," the visual object helps readers quickly understand relationships among the behavioral nodes illustrated. Besides that, the Land of Oz is alive and active in every poker room (and business organization!) in the world, so it serves us well to become familiar with its occupants.

SIX BEHAVIORAL NODES

Four major characters from the Land of Oz are shown on the matrix in Figure 9–1: Scarecrow, Tin Man, Wizard, and Lion. Each of these characters is associated with points on four of the six behavioral nodes on the diagram (out of hundreds, or even thousands, we could have selected). The behavioral nodes are shown with opposite polar extreme points at either end of the axis. The nodes are (clockwise from upper left):

1. *Facts* (upper left) and *Opinions* (lower right). Some people are influenced by facts; some by opinions. Factual people tend toward using analytical methods (experiments, measurement, testing, logic, etc.); opinion people tend toward using political methods (coercion, consensus building, propaganda, emotional appeals, etc.)

2. *Substance* (upper left) and *Illusion* (lower right). Some people are more influenced by what can be seen and touched; some by what can be seen and imagined.

3. *Reasoned Aggression* (north point) and *Over-the-top Aggression* (south point). Some people use aggression at selected times with reasonable (but not necessarily gentle) force applied relative to value of objective and nature of situation; some people will throw in everything they have without regard to relative value or situation.

4. *Change* (upper right) and *Stasis* (lower left). Some people are willing to accept change; others are only comfortable with the current situation.

5. *Ideas* (upper right) and *Rules* (lower left). Some people can utilize ideas and concepts to govern choices; others can only be satisfied with governance by rules and precedence.

6. *Seek Gain/Opportunity* (east point) and *Avoid Loss/Mistake* (west point). Some people move in the direction of perceived benefit; some people move away from perceived threat. This is one of the more powerful and most reliable behavioral nodes.

FOUR OZ-TYPE CHARACTERS

♦ The *Scarecrow* (Analyst) resides in the upper left quadrant. The Scarecrow is an analytic person. He measures, sorts, categorizes, and compares evidence to prevent himself from making major errors. He makes reasonable judgments and tends to risk his money in proportion to rewards. The Scarecrow is likely to be selective in his choice of hands to play, while limiting his aggression to situations in which he calculates he has the best hand. A Scarecrow will bluff selectively and semi-bluff only with draws that are likely to win hands if he hits his draw and a showdown becomes necessary. Chris Ferguson is an example of a scarecrow.

♦ The *Lion* (Bureaucrat) occupies the lower left quadrant. The Lion is a worried individual. He has achieved some kind of status or notoriety in his world and is afraid it will be taken from him. He feels outcomes should be governed by rules and guidelines that respect and guard his position in the hierarchy. When threatened, the Lion will react emotionally and is capable of extreme behavior aimed at intimidating others. The Lion believes he deserves to win. He may play erratically, sometimes loose, sometimes tight. Because of his emotional sensitivity, the Lion seems to be tilted easily. But be cautious, the Lion is king of the forest because he is a crafty hunter with long claws and sharp teeth, and he intends to defend his position. Phil Helmuth and Mike Matusow are examples of Lions.

♦ The *Tin Man* (Executive) inhabits the upper right quadrant. The Tin Man is open to ideas and change and will actively seek opportunities that are available. The Tin Man takes risk and is more interested in outcomes than statistics. He will try to understand people around him, and then use his understanding to manipulate them—but in a generally friendly way. He means no harm; at the same time, he carries an ax, which he can use effectively. The Tin Man wants to win, but winning does not define him. Rather, he seeks to be effective at what he does. Winning is a way of validating effectiveness. The Tin Man values consensus and will not try to dominate a situation if that is the best way for him to win. Joe Hachem and Jamie Gold are examples of Tin Men.

♦ The *Wizard* (Politician) lives in the lower right quadrant. The Wizard is a dangerous, self-confident player who reads others very effectively. The Wizard wears a façade of friendly openness which masks a keen desire to dominate and wield power. The Wizard is a talker, a social animal. One of his most effective tools is his ability to convince others around him that he has their best interests at heart. The Wizard depends on illusion to keep others off-guard and off-balance. He seeks opinions in order to position himself where he can control outcomes without placing himself at risk. The Wizard can be loose and aggressive in his play, but he knows what he is doing. Daniel Negreanu is an example of a wizard.

No person is purely one type or another. In the way of illustration, we have placed the names of six poker pros where *we think* they might belong. These guys are the best of the best so far as playing poker is concerned, but each one wins using a different set of techniques. Our objective in presenting the analytical framework above is to introduce the idea of analyzing and thinking about the characters you meet at the poker table and in the conference room in a more organized fashion.

Taking the time to figure out who you are dealing with in a competitive situation will go a long way toward helping you to gain an edge. The real issue, then, is how do you make an effective evaluation of a player's behavior? How do you figure out where a person might be on the Oz matrix? And, how do you use that information to take their money at poker or win the day in business, career, wealth, power, and relationship areas of life. In Chapter 10, we will give you a technique for quickly uncovering the essence of other people's playing styles.

10

Getting to Know You

IT'S THURSDAY afternoon. You allow yourself a virtual moment to slip into your favorite familiar fantasy and wander into a casino off the Vegas strip. An aromatic haze of tobacco smoke mixed with the effluvium of human effort, the fragrance of fantasy, and the barest hint of consequences, impart an ambience of slick success and easy gains to the place.

The cheerful ding-a-ling of casino slot machines, like a tireless chorus of pulsating mechanical munchkins, offers a song of praise to the gods of profit worshipped within that cathedral of greed, that magical neon-flash netherworld that represents America at the absolute pinnacle of capitalist evolution. The quiet whisper of cards deftly propelled across the green felt of a Blackjack table suggests the seductive swish of naked legs caressing satin sheets, or maybe the silken slither of masked figures dressed in multihued ecclesiastical robes distributing eucharist in some ancient pagan celebration.

A naked figure of lady luck sits frozen in marble ecstasy before the keyboard of an overly shiny black piano once played—in an undoubtedly golden, but absolutely forgotten time—by Frank Sinatra. A cacophony of money in the making, a splash of sin in the selling, a riot of fun in the having, all rush the senses with a pleasant lust for games and chance, love and luck, as you walk through the binge and bustle toward the inner sanctum of the poker room.

When you enter the poker room, a boothling instantly estimates your worth, head to toe, top to bottom, from his perch behind a small desk, the sharply irritating odor of pseudo-importance he exudes dilates your nostrils and waters your eyes as you approach. (Boothlings are minor cathedral clerics who occupy space and create problems for otherwise enthusiastic casino faithful. They are related in IQ and behavior to the mechanical munchkins noted above [that is, they make noise, take money, and seldom pay off]. Unlike the munchkins, however, they cannot be eliminated when they misbehave, just promoted to management. Further, they do not "ding" if you pull an arm.)

You can see from his scarcely suppressed grimace that your rating is hardly that of a slug; he could care less if you live or die. But your being this close to a person who may have talked personally with Phil Helmuth, or at the very least has seen Phil in the flesh, plucks a harmonic chord in your mind. "Can I help you?" he asks in his best, eager-less, "I-hope-not" tone.

"I want to play poker," you manage to whisper, almost overwhelmed by the prospect of actually stroking the cards.

"OK," the boothling answers, his accent placing him from somewhere near Peoria, Illinois. "What kind of poker?"

"What you got?" you blurt nervously.

"Do you like limit or no limit?"

"Uh, limit, maybe?"

"High limit or low limit?"

"What's the difference?"

"In high limit, you lose a lot. In low limit, you lose less."

"I better start with low limit."

"Good thinking," he snorts. "Lucky you. We have a seat on table 12, $5/$10 Limit Hold 'em.'"

You walk over to your seat and look around as you start stacking chips on the table. The dealer says, "This is Don. He is joining our table, let's welcome him," like it was some kind of Sunday morning Toastmasters meeting. A few people at the table seem to say, "Hello." With all the background noise, though, the words sound suspiciously like, "Buzz off!" or a similar R-rated appellation.

An old guy in a soiled white cowboy hat and fake Indian turquoise-silver string tie smiles a kind welcome, belches, then farts, but not loudly at all. The fat twenty-something at the end of the table sneers maliciously, adjusts his White Sox baseball cap, and leans over a chair back displaying his slightly greenish underwear. He is bouncing what appears to be a wad of hundred dollar bills wrapped in rubber bands impatiently on the table. The harlequin bug odor emanating from your right is a woman who seems to have applied several competing layers of fluorescent spray paint to her face in a vainglorious attempt to resurrect long desiccated youth. There are also a couple of nondescript white guys sucking their teeth in boredom and another fellow who vaguely resembles Gus Hansen. Or is it Phil Ivey? Or maybe Johnny Chan? Something about the eyes.

"And this is the glamorous world of the professional poker player (or high finance, or Big Six consulting, or what have you . . . fill in the blank)?" you wonder as you glance at the hole cards in front of you.

"Check or bet!" the dealer chants. "Check that debt!"

"Check that debt ratio." The dealer sounds strangely burbled. "Don, wake up. What's that debt ratio? Get your mind in the game, buddy."

Oh no, it's not the dealer, nor is this place lovely, lascivious Las Vegas. It's Harold Brine, the company controller at the weekly finance committee meeting. It's certainly not a poker game either, but as you look around the conference table, you realize that the players are the same. Here you are (at least in your dreams): an under-paid, over-educated business wizard; and your peers and coworkers walked straight out of a Star Wars bar. How ironic for you.

Given what you have to work with, it may not be easy to work up much enthusiasm for gaining an intimate knowledge of your fellow poker players' character attributes, or even those of your coworkers, but it is absolutely necessary. Further, no matter how normal you consider yourself, others do not look at you the same way—not now, not ever. They see you through their own lens of reality, their own special prism, which distorts you and the rest of the world to fit its particular version of things as they are, or should be. There is one ultimate reality on this highly amusing plane of existence. Everyone believes he is the hero of the play. Remember this point always: In dealing with people, the movie is about ME! Everyone else, including YOU, is a bit player.

Hence, the greater your willingness and ability to understand and appreciate reality under the terms and conditions of your comrades and competitors, the better your chances of winning the game. The key to winning is to integrate your understanding of others and your understanding of yourself with accurate and objective observations and estimates of current external realities to develop workable tactics designed to realize practical short-term goals that, when added together, will eventually arrive at your ultimate long-term objective (whatever that objective may be.)

Sun Tzu says, "If you know your enemy and you know yourself, you will not lose in one hundred battles." The more often you step outside yourself and attempt to perceive your feelings and actions as others would (let us say, by using a cross-section of other-typed persons, one from each Oz-type quadrant), the better you will understand yourself. The better you understand yourself, the more easily you will be able to decipher the actions of others as they relate to you and to external stimuli. It is a continuous circle. Know yourself better, know your enemy better. Know your enemy better, know yourself better. Self-realization is neither easy nor entertaining, but it is the ultimate tool for competitive success.

Type Casting with Sonar

Sonar is a system that detects unseen underwater objects (like schools of fish) by emitting short pulses of sound, which are reflected off an object and echoed back. The reflected sound is then measured to provide information about the size of the object and its distance from the sonar transmitter/receiver. The short pulses of high frequency sound are called "pings." We will use the keyword P-I-N-G to describe the technique for identifying the OZ-type characteristics of an individual and using the characteristics to group an individual into one of the Oz-type quadrants (Scarecrow, Lion, Tin Man, or Wizard). Just like a sonar device locates a school of fish, you "ping" people to discover their behavioral characteristics. P-I-N-G is a process for identifying behavioral characteristics and positioning people according to the Oz-type matrix.

The four activities represented by the keyword P-I-N-G are:

Pose

Inquire

e**N**gage

Group

You could also, if you choose, use the same process to group people into any other behavioral or personality matrix you might select. It will work independently of the particular organizational system employed to classify people. The method for obtaining information remains the same.

POSE

Every sonar device needs a stable and constant internal reference point. Without a stable reference point, the device has no way to accurately measure the distance and shape of objects it encounters.

Take yourself back to the poker table in our daydream above. Instead of approaching the table, however, imagine you are already seated at the table and you are watching yourself walk toward it. What do you see? Think about this very, very closely. Can you clearly imagine how you would look to someone else as you walk up to the poker table? (If you cannot, videotape yourself walking around the room and review the file. We guarantee, unless you are quite used to seeing yourself on TV, that this exercise will be both surprising and uncomfortable.)

The way you look to others is your *pose*. A consistent, reliable pose, which you have selected for yourself, is an absolute first step in accurately pinging others. The necessity of self-selection of your own pose gets back to some of the earliest points in this book. Your behavioral traits and your persona have developed over the years as a reaction to many conflicting, friendly and not-so-friendly external events. Unless you have practiced making yourself into what you desire yourself to be, you are an uncoordinated accumulation of past failures, successes, criticisms, attitudes, beliefs, and fears.

Intentional success comes to those who practice self-worth and self-selection. Take a moment right now to think about choosing a pose you like, perhaps that of an admired role model. Acquire a video of your role model in action and practice his or her walk and talk until you can emulate it naturally. Start using the new pose without telling anyone. Notice how others react, particularly those you know well.

Adopting a consistent pose provides the necessary stable reference point required to measure the response of people when you enter a situation. If you *know* how you appear when you walk across a room, you can gauge others' response to you. You will know whether they are attracted to your pose or intimidated by it. This kind of information is priceless because most individuals have no idea that they are giving it up.

INQUIRE

Sit down at our fantasy poker table once again. Reach out and restack your chips a moment. Relax. Breathe in and out slowly. Internalize the ambience of the casino; hear it, see it, feel it. Soon you will turn to the person on your left and start a conversation. How would you do that without letting her know that you are probing for her innermost secrets? (If you feel that this little exercise is just a bit over the top, think again. Do you want to win the pot or just be a chip [or chump] for others to play with as they pursue rewards for themselves? Take a moment and try it! It's not a game. This type of mental playacting *will*—not *could*, *not* should, not *can*—change your life.)

The idea is to break the I-C-E with the other person.

....

You break the I-C-E by:

Stimulating **I**magination

Arousing **C**uriosity

Establishing **E**mpathy

....

You can stimulate *imagination,* arouse *curiosity,* and establish *empathy* most effectively by asking the right kind of questions. Questions are the most powerful tool for opening a relationship.

What kind of question do you ask first? Obviously, you should ask a question that the other person, under normal circumstances, will feel completely comfortable answering. However, start by asking permission. "Can I ask you a question?" or "Would you mind if I asked your opinion about something?" Then continue with a question about poker or another subject you have confidence the two of you have in common and would not be considered controversial.

These opening questions must be scripted and practiced to the point they sound perfectly natural when asked. Further, since tone of voice and facial expression carry much of the meaning in conversation, practice asking the questions in front of a mirror until your face and voice convey nothing but innocent interest.

ENGAGE

Once your opening has been completed and you are on speaking terms with your target, your objective is quickly to evaluate them and place them into one of the four Oz-type categories. You can do this by paying attention to their speech patterns and physical actions as you casually converse. For speech patterns we will use the keyword T-A-L-K, and for physical actions we will use the keyword M-E-L-T.

···

The speech patterns represented by the keyword T-A-L-K are:

Tension

Aggression

Language

Key/Tone

···

The physical actions represented by the keyword M-E-L-T are:

Motion

Eyes

Lips

Tremble

···

The two grouping keywords used here are but a small part of the science of uncovering other people's characteristics from their speech and movement. However, as with most of the keywords discussed in this book, learning a little and then practicing what you learn will open the doors to further progress.

♦ In the keyword T-A-L-K, **Tension** refers to how tight or loose a person appears to be. Tight people may be nervous, suspicious, or uncertain. Loose people are less concerned with protecting themselves and more with interacting with the environment.

♦ **Aggression** refers the tendency to try to dominate. If the individual tries to dominate the conversation with you, he may also try to dominate the game. Attempt to determine whether the individual is an offensive or defensive aggressor. Is he aggressive because he is afraid (defensive) or predatory (offensive)? Calm is *not* the opposite of aggressive. A very strong, aggressive player may be quite calm while he sizes up the situation.

♦ **Language** is critical to understanding background. Even a highly polished individual has difficulty hiding all verbal evidence of his background. Words and accents can reveal place of origin, household status, and level of education if one listens carefully. Language usage, however, can be modified greatly by an experienced actor or con artist to create false impressions. The use of anger or crude and inappropriate language is usually an intentional attempt to impress, upset, or distract others.

♦ **Key/Tone** refers to the pitch and tenor of the person's voice. Does the voice seem squeezed? Is he speaking unusually fast or slow? Does she seem distracted or overly involved? Is he enunciating words or slurring them?

First impressions are important to you. We have learned from childhood to size up people within a few seconds of first meeting them. Follow your impressions, they are seldom far off. If the other person seems warm and friendly but dangerous, stay on your guard.

♦ For evaluating actions, in keyword M-E-L-T, **Motion** refers to the way a person gestures, smiles, frowns, rocks, or crosses his arms. It includes any of the little, mostly unconscious, activities that accompany conversation among people. Watch for facial expressions and gestures that are coincident with words spoken, such as a forced smile or sudden hand movement, for confirmation or denial of the meaning of spoken words.

Be aware that everyone who plays poker will try to give misleading tells. Most are crude and easily spotted because occasional players do not practice these devices. For instance, a person who scratches his head and generally tries to behave befuddled when making a bet is probably not confused at all.

♦ Subtle physical actions are more reliable indicators because they cannot be counterfeited without skill. **Eye** movements are for the most part involuntary. When you see something you like, your pupils will dilate to let more light in. Serious players wear sunglasses to prevent observation of eye movement. When you converse with others, watch how the eyes move for indications of interest or indications of disagreement. If you bring up a disagreeable subject, you should be able to note a difference in their response (a squint perhaps) from their reaction to something they find pleasant. Watch and learn.

◆ A person's **Lips** also provide reliable clues. When someone is frustrated or angry, the lips tend to purse or tighten. Even a slight, momentary tightening of the lips is a sign that some aspect of the current situation has touched their sensitivities.

◆ A **Tremble** of the hands or lips is difficult to hide. When people get a surge of adrenaline through their bodies because of anger, fear, or intense excitement, they will tremble. Trembling can be caused by several common physical disorders. It can also be faked rather convincingly. Depending on whom you are dealing with, assess trembling hands or lips carefully.

GROUP

After conversing with an individual for a few minutes, you should be able to place them into one of the Oz-type categories. Again, trust your instincts when reading character. You have a lifetime of experience already. Go with your gut.

To briefly review the categories in the Oz matrix:

Scarecrow: Analyst, Facts, Substance, Reasoned Aggression, Avoid Mistake/Loss

Tin Man: Executive, Change, Ideas, Reasoned Aggression, Seek Opportunity/Gain

Lion: Bureaucrat, Rules, Stasis, Over-the-Top Aggression, Avoid Mistake/Loss

Wizard: Politician, Illusion, Opinions, Over-the-Top Aggression, Seek Opportunity/Gain

♠ ♣ ♡ ◇

11

Pre-Flop Concepts

MOST TEXAS Hold 'em books argue that your choice of opening hands is the most influential decision you make when you play. We tend to agree that opening-hand selection sets the stage for all ensuing decisions and, as such, it influences the possibilities you may be presented with. Playing opening hands effectively builds a solid foundation for the remainder of the hand.

But opening hands are only as good as you play them. For instance, we have observed that many people overplay AK, particularly AKo (where o = off-suit; s = suited). AK is a wonderful drawing hand which stands up well against every other type of opening hand except perhaps really big pairs (AA, KK). If the flop does not help your AK, however, in the face of a strong bet, it is probably wise to consider laying the hand down. The same logic applies to other good drawing hands. If the flop does not help your hand, consider laying them down because any small pair can and will beat a draw.

There is a tendency, particularly in small stake limit games, to deflate opening-hand standards as the game proceeds, particularly if you are hitting crazy flops and raking in piles of chips, or conversely, you are not hitting anything and frustration is creeping in. You may have watched professional players opening and winning with garbage hands on TV. Further, you will observe players at your own table winning large pots with small pairs, small to middle connectors, or with even more ridiculous combinations. The temptation, at this point, is to try emulating someone like Daniel Negreanu, who often opens pots with mid-valued connectors. Playing opening card combinations outside your level of competence and experience usually results in additional losses, so rein in your emotions.

 "Connectors" are any two unpaired cards which can form part of a straight.

The sage advice from experienced players is to develop and stick with (as a starting point for developing technique and ability) a set of starting hands that will put you somewhere into the range of 25 percent of pots. (*Note:* this range will always result in your playing too tight when up against *highly skilled* players, but against loose and aggressive wannabes, it will hold up well!) This set of starting hands does not necessarily include those hands you play from the blinds when you are getting good pot odds (because you may end up playing some strange hands from the blinds). Playing in the 25-percent range tends to be more profitable for the novice player because you will not be chasing after so many potentially losing unsuited combinations after the flop, while you are still somewhat uncertain about how to play more sophisticated situations. On the other hand, you will not be playing so tight that other players will take advantage of you all the time (just some of the time).

Hold 'em is a difficult game, which always tests the spirit. Winning is wonderful; losing is painful. The only way to beat the game is to accept and practice the discipline needed to survive both good luck and bad luck in their turn. If, in the end, you walk away from the Hold 'em tables a net winner, you will have truly accomplished something worthwhile.

Evaluating Opening Hands with the POCKET Score

Our objective for the POCKET Score process was to develop a starting-hand evaluation methodology that quickly and easily approximates the relative strength of a given starting hand. The number computed using the POCKET Score process described here gives you a rough reference point for evaluating the relative weakness or strength against other players. The score is easy to calculate. Just look at your two pocket cards and then use the following point table to sum up the POCKET Score for a given hand:

Ace	15 points
King	13 points
Queen	12 points
Jack	11 points
Ten	10 points
Nine	9 points
Eight	8 points
Seven	7 points
Six	6 points
Five	5 points
Four	4 points
Three	3 points
Two	2 points
Pair	add 40 points Premium for pairs AA to TT
	add 35 points Premium for pairs 77, 88, 99
	add 30 points Premium for pairs 44, 55, 66
Suited	add 20 points Premium
ATo to JTo	add 20 points Premium (*Broadway* off-suit)
A9o to A5o	add 15 points Premium
K9o to K7o	add 15 points Premium

Q9o to Q8o	add 15 points Premium
J9o; T9o; 98o	add 15 points Premium

 "Broadway" cards are those between Ace and Ten. A Broadway straight is Ace to Ten.

Note: In our opinion, pocket-card combinations below those listed in the tables are highly speculative hands under almost every circumstance. Hands with lower scores will win less than 50 percent of the time against one other random hand.

Here are a few examples of computations:

The POCKET Score for AA is 15(A) + 15(A) + 40 (Broadway pair) = 70. The percentage of time a pair of Aces will win against two random hands held to the river is about 73 percent.

The POCKET Score for AKo is 15(A) + 13(K) + 20 (Broadway off-suit) = 48. The percentage of time AKo will win against two random hands held to the river is about 48 percent.

The POCKET Score for T9s is 10(T) + 9(9) + 20(Suited) = 39. The percentage of time T9s will win against two random hands held to the river is about 39 percent.

The POCKET Score for 66 is 6(6) + 6(6) + 30(small Pair) = 42.

The POCKET Score tells you whether you have a relatively strong hand or a relatively weak hand. If your hand scores 40 or more points, you have a relatively strong hand. Scores of 34 to 39 are average hands, which may not be strong enough to play against hands that have been raised by early position players (see discussion of position below). Hands that score below 34 should be avoided except where pot odds justify playing a hand that is known to be weak.

If you just play hands scoring 40 or above, you will play the strongest 20 percent of hands dealt, but you will find that playing so few hands may not provide an optimal mix for profitability.

Experiment with the mix of hands you play until you find one that is comfortable. For example, although the POCKET Scores are somewhat lower, we have added 87s, 76s, and 65s to our opening hands table because these combinations play well (when they hit the flop) against high pairs and other high card combinations. Appendix B contains opening-hand tables, POCKET Scores, and expected percentages of the number of opening hands played.

Evaluating Pre-Flop Position

Pre-flop position in Texas Hold 'em refers to the place you are sitting relative to the dealer, who is the player with the button (a white disk with the word "dealer" written on it) in front of him. The dealer button moves one player to the left after each hand, so the position of each player relative to the dealer button changes with each hand. The strongest theoretical position prior to the flop is the player *with* the dealer button in front of him because he will act last on all future betting rounds for that given hand. Acting last gives him the advantage of knowing what other players in the hand have decided to do before he needs to act.

We would argue that there are actually two pre-flop positions that offer the opportunity to leverage opponents: the *dealer position* discussed above; and the under-the-gun position. The *under-the-gun* position is the person who acts first on that round of betting. Almost all poker books recommend betting from the under-the-gun position pre-flop only if you have a very strong opening hand (upper 40s and higher POCKET Scores using our scoring system).

If you follow the standard advice to the letter, of course, you will be telegraphing the strength of your hand to everyone else at the table. Raising from the under-the-gun position, however, almost always puts the other players into a defensive posture. They will not know whether you are following the "book" (starting with a very strong hand) or faking it. Their uncertainty gives you an advantage. Calling the blind from the under-the-gun position also creates uncertainty because calling in early position will be viewed as a weak bet. By varying your moves under-the-gun—raise at times, call at times, bet standard opening hands, bet substandard hands; that is, by mixing up your actions unpredictably—you will be able to create a feeling of uncertainty in others.

Uncertainty in others is the raw material of opportunity for you. Uncertainty gives you a powerful edge. Your objective at the table is to create such a strong aura of uncertainty around your actions that people will become highly indecisive when they are facing a bet from you. When people are indecisive, you can move them around wherever and whenever you want. If you are able to move others at will, but remain fixed, strong, and confident yourself, you have the keys to winning at any game you play.

Betting Before the Flop

There are three purposes to betting before the flop:

1. *Betting allows you to see the flop and possibly continue in the hand.*

2. *Betting allows you to send a message to other players.* The message you are able to send depends upon how receptive your audience is. For instance, it is always easier to bluff a good player than a poor player. A poor player will not be able to evaluate the possibilities inherent in the cards and will not appreciate your message.

3. *You can use the pre-flop bet to reduce the size of the field.* Reducing the number of players you face is immensely important because your odds of winning a hand decrease significantly with each additional player who sees the flop. Getting just one more person to fold pre-flop will help you increase your average winnings significantly.

In Low Limit Hold 'em games, your ability to use the pre-flop bet to reduce the field is questionable. (They do not call it "No-fold 'em Hold 'em" for nothing. In a typical Vegas casino $2/$4 Limit game, the average number of people seeing each and every flop can approach 5 or 6 out of 9.) Players do not consider calling a bet of less than $20 to $40 important money. (After all, you cannot buy a hamburger in Caesar's Palace for less than $20.) Often when you raise a blind pre-flop, you will create a rush to enter the pot because weaker players will only consider how much they might win as a result of the number of bets in the pot. For Low Limit games, you *must* be able to make the best hand every time you bet. It's that or get out with four or five people looking at every pot.

In No Limit games, it may be possible to bet enough pre-flop to begin to discourage players from entering the pot. However, betting inflation has occurred even in lower blind No Limit games (such as $1/$3). Because of betting inflation, it becomes harder and harder to use the pre-flop raise to drive people out, even when raising to ridiculous levels. In sessions where it is possible, you might try really overbetting your premium hands to avoid recurrent episodes of trying to outrun weak hands held by weak players with full wallets and empty heads. But an overbetting strategy may not work because many players also consider large opening bets a sign of weakness. They will associate a large opening bet with a middle pair, or something like AJ. Further, premium hands are rare, so you will end up playing suboptimally tight. We have seen many of the better players in Vegas refuse to play anything lower than $20/$40 Limit and $2/$5 No Limit games to avoid losing the ability to bet good hands for value.

For a given Hold 'em session, experiment with different amounts to try to determine what level of bet gives the results you want. If you simply cannot drive people out of a hand, then develop an intermediate strategy. For example (in No Limit games), you can bet enough to make it worthwhile to win the hand if others call or raise the bet, something like two times the big blind, but not so much that you get overly involved when the flop is unfavorable (which will happen quite often). Or, perhaps, you might just call all your acceptable opening hands, see the flops, and try to trap other players when you hit your cards and fold or bluff when you do not.

The experience gained from experimenting with different opening strategies will pay off. You will quickly begin to see how changing your opening play also changes the way other players respond to you. Work it out until you have evolved a reasonable balance (for you) between risk and reward. The trapping strategy (which is a form of bluffing from strength) is very popular these days in casino tournament play, especially when players hold AA or KK. Be alert for traps whenever a player simply calls the flop and turn, particularly in the face of an aggressive bet by a previous player, or when a player opens the pot with a raise of exactly three times the big blind (especially if they have shown themselves to be careful in other hands).

Flirting with Opportunity

Building a decision model for predicting outcomes in interpersonal competition can be tricky. The task involves identifying and measuring critical variables which are relevant to the outcomes desired, based on whatever scant or unreliable information might be available at the outset of a situation or project. Very few people are able to do this effectively. As with Hold 'em, even if you consistently practice great opening hand strategy, the fall of the cards combined with the play of the hand dictates your level of success. Competitive situations from business, career, wealth, power, and relationship areas of life involve even more factors than a hand of Hold 'em, so making broad generalizations about how to predict success in these areas will be useful only in a strictly limited sense.

Returning to one of the major themes of this book, as a human being, whether you are aware of the models you are using or not, you will employ models to make decisions. Modeling is the mechanism used by nature to allow us to make decisions when faced with previously unknown factors and circumstances (which is often). As we pointed out earlier in the text, most of the time we do not select the models we use throughout life; they are conveniently, but not always effectively, provided by our experiences, our parents, our education, our culture, and our environment. As a consequence, they are often highly inadequate when we face situations that are not within the (relatively) narrow confines of the constraints set by the assumptions used to build the model.

You can clearly see how the inadequacies of home-grown, accidentally sown decision models might hamper effective decision making when you are faced with an opportunity that does not fit into one of the models you now utilize. If your model is effective enough, if it screens out ideas and concepts that are not useful to you (based on the assumptions of your model), when you inevitably run into something the model does not recognize or interpret well, you simply will not see it, even if it could be highly beneficial or highly dangerous to you. It is for this reason that most kinds of opportunity pass us by in a cloud of dust. We just do not see the possibilities because we screen them out.

How do we selectively change the parameters of internal programming sufficiently and effectively enough to recognize potentially useful, but unfamiliar, concepts? Changing internal parameters and guidelines is one of the few methods available to us that provide a viable and realistic chance for significant improvement in our performance during interpersonal competitive situations. In Hold 'em, this might mean, for example, recognizing we may play certain hands in less than optimal fashion and seeking the information we need to learn to play them differently. (People are often strongly resistant to the possibility that they may be doing something that is less than adequate when it comes to playing poker. It is easier, but less profitable, to believe that luck or opinion or the weather or something else outside your control is running against you.)

S-P-A-C-E

To initiate the process of creating a change that will give us a chance to advance, use the keyword S-P-A-C-E.

The concepts in the keyword S-P-A-C-E are:

Specifications

People

Advantage

Compensation

Evolution

By examining the *space* around a situation or idea, we can begin to explore the shape and dynamics of things we would previously have dismissed or simply relegated to the trash bin because we are using a type of model that eliminates certain possibilities. If you will practice this short exercise *once a day,* we guarantee that you will begin to see ideas and events in a way you did not in the past. Just take a look at some idea, some concept, or some event from another angle once a day. Seeing ideas and events differently will lead with certainty to your uncovering ways to improve your performance in competitive situations. Make a change; give yourself a chance.

Specifications means facts and details. Make an attempt to uncover the real dimensions of an idea. In today's world, we are spoiled by the overwhelming quantity of information available. We tend to ingest a large amount of information in small sound or picture bites, like the evening news. We read a headline, grasp the idea, and move on to the next. Get into the detail about something that interests you or something you are not familiar with. Understand what is going on—exactly, not through the spin of the news media and politically biased experts.

People drive ideas and situations. Who is involved here? Who initiated the situation? Who is pursuing it? Who could be involved behind the scenes? How are these people related? How are the people related to you? Does their interest project a trend or change in a fundamental process?

Advantage, or benefit, fuels the interest of people. How does the idea you are looking at create an advantage for the people you identified? How does opposing the idea create an advantage for those who are against the idea? How could this situation benefit you? Is it possible there is something in the idea that others may have overlooked, or are trying to hide?

Compensation turns advantage into tangible currency. Currency is any form of benefit which can be transferred from one person to another. Cash is the most obvious form, but there are many other forms of currency available in the world with which to pay compensation. (Sex and influence come quickly to mind; usually, however, the trail will lead back to money. In this wonderful, fascinating world, with money, you can acquire as much sex and influence as you need—megalomaniacs excepted.) What type of compensation is being paid? How much currency is involved? How is payment arranged? Who makes payment?

Evolution relates to the way in which the idea may grow and the implications of its growth or rejection. Can you see how the idea or project may proceed? Are there implications in this evolution? Does it affect you? Can it benefit you?

The effort that you make to explore the space around ideas, events, concepts, projects, and people will pay big dividends. You will begin to do this analysis automatically. When you begin to process events through the S-P-A-C-E model, you will see connections and opportunities that were not apparent before. When you smell an opportunity in the future, you may actually be able to track down the source and take advantage of it.

PART THREE

KINETICS

One of the fundamental principles of tactics in competition is deception. Sun Tzu said: "The essence of tactics is deceiving the enemy." The primary tool used to deceive or mislead an opponent is his own perceptive model. As we noted in Chapter 11, if your model of reality does not consider a certain idea or concept relevant, you will not see it. Hence, the initial goal of Part Three, Kinetics, is the development of an effective and organized approach to evaluating the circumstances you actually face. Preconceived notions of how to play a hand or gain an advantage must be set aside in favor of objective analysis of the situation as it really exists (i.e., situational reality). You must see reality if you are to win consistently.

♤ ♧ ♡ ♢

12

Evaluating the Flop
I. Reading Pocket Cards

THE FLOP represents a turning point in the play of a Hold 'em hand and gives us a convenient analogy to similar critical points during interpersonal competition. Using our Poker Paradigm as a reference model, the flop moves the competitive process from preparation and positioning to engagement and maneuver. Over the next few chapters, using the keyword S-W-O-R-D, we will discuss the elements of tactics to be employed under different conditions once the engagement has begun.

In terms of Texas Hold 'em, the flop both enlarges and limits the possibilities inherent in the first two pocket cards. In terms of competitive situations from business, career, wealth, power, and relationship areas of life, the transition from positioning to maneuver enlarges the number of tactical choices, but quickly limits flexibility once movement has started. Within this context, we will discuss the selection and application of tactics for gaining advantage over your competition under a variety of competitive situations.

The flop consists of three cards. Each flop has its own unique fabric, or texture as it is often called. Evaluating the flop involves two steps. First (and you will do this part instinctively), you must assess the impact of the flop on your own hand. Second, you must assess the possible impact of the flop on your opponents' possible hands in relation to yours. In order to make the assessment, you will need to make a reasonable guess at what other players are holding. As effectively as you can, you need to read their hands and their minds.

Reading other players' hands is always a major concern in Hold 'em. The better you can read hands, the more successful you will be. In the remainder of this chapter, we will develop a method which will make it extremely easy for you to pinpoint a range of pocket cards in other players' hands. In Chapters 13 and 14, we will show you how to use our pocket card reading method to analyze and determine the value of different kinds of flops.

Reading Pocket Cards

At the time of the flop, you have two useful bits of information. First, you know how much other players who are still participating in the hand have bet before the flop. Second, you can approximate the majority of players' pre-flop starting hand criteria fairly accurately.

Pre-flop betting patterns used during a unique hand—particularly, the timing of calls, raises, re-raises, and check-raises—communicate players' opinions about the relative strength of pocket card holdings. If you think carefully about a hand of Texas Hold 'em, betting is the only action a player absolutely needs to perform in order to talk with other players. Within the limits of the game, betting says everything. Other sorts of communication at the table are unnecessary.

Using betting patterns to read a player's hand must be done with awareness of the pitfalls. Since betting patterns are the primary means of communicating, they are also the primary means of creating deception. Hence, the predictive value of pre-flop betting patterns varies greatly from player-to-player and hand-to-hand. For example, we have noticed a trend toward slow-playing AA and KK in Vegas casino tournament play (that is, simply calling these premium hands before the flop to set a trap). Therefore, a player who suddenly turns into a calling station, after previously exhibiting normal calling and raising patterns, should be suspected immediately.

 To "slow-play" is to bet a very strong hand in a weak manner in order to set a strong hand trap.

The most important information you get from the fact that another player is willing to see the flop is based on the fact that the great majority of players use similar distributions of starting hands in deciding to enter pots. If you were to survey the literature of Texas Hold 'em, you would find little difference among authors (including us) regarding the general distribution of recommended starting hands.

We all learn almost identical starting-hand distributions when we start playing Hold 'em. While players tend to expand starting-hand distributions as they gain experience, very few players are willing to play a large number of hands starting with any two random cards. (Why? Because you will lose a lot of dough unless you are extremely skilled and clever at playing after the flop, or the people you are playing against are totally unaware. Neither of these conditions are common in real life.) Almost any sensible set of criteria used to narrow starting hands down from any two cards results in a distribution of hands falling into a range of 25 to 35 percent of total starting hands.

More importantly, the expected value of a given hand that you may hold varies little whether your opponent's distribution is fairly tight or fairly loose. As a result, you do not need to spend a lot of effort trying to "put your opponent on a hand"—you already know what he probably has. And, it matters very little if you are slightly wrong (we understand that in high stakes limit games, this "very little" can actually be the source of your edge. If you are going to play high stakes limit games, get your black belt in Hold 'em first), so long as your opponent is using a reasonable range of possible distributions.

Here is an example of what we are talking about. Assume you are heads-up on the flop with another player, and you are holding KQ (hearts) in the pocket. Against a player who plays a starting hand distribution that includes 30 percent of possible pocket hands, you will win 55 percent of the time if you are holding a KQ (hearts or any other suit). Against a player who plays 20 percent of possible starting hands you will win 51 percent of the time. The decision-making value of the KQ (hearts) for you versus these two distributions is virtually equal, even though a 30-percent distribution contains 400 possible hands and a 20-percent distribution contains only 270 hands. Your KQ (hearts) will win 51 to 55 percent of the time. There is not enough difference in how well you do against either set of starting hands, at reasonable limits, for you to be overly concerned about which one is actually being used.

We feel highly confident making the assumption that a significant majority of players will play starting-hand distributions which are limited to a range of about 25 to 35 percent of possible starting hands. For instance, if you were to use the Pocket Score system described in Chapter 11, playing hands with scores of 40 and above includes about 21 percent of hands; playing hands with scores of 33 and above (and these are all hands which will yield a statistical advantage against two other random hands played to showdown) includes about 35 percent of hands—a fairly loose set of starting hands by many standards.

The conclusion here is this: If a player is in the hand with you *at all*, he has a very high likelihood of holding cards from a distribution of hands that is well known to you and that has fairly low sensitivity with respect to the expected value of your hand against those distributions. Further, the wider the distribution of your opponents' starting hands, the larger the expected value of your own hand and the greater your overall advantage from playing a sensibly limited range of starting hands.

Starting-Hand Distribution Analysis

In what way do starting hand distributions differ as they become wider? They certainly do not differ at the stronger end of the distributions. Let's take a quick look at a 15-percent distribution first because we believe that almost everyone, even a super-glue tight player, is willing (given position and betting factors) to employ a starting-hand distribution that encompasses a minimum of 15 percent of possible starting hands.

A strong **15-percent distribution** would be:

Pairs: AA to 77 (48 hands)

Suited Aces: AKs to A7s (28 hands)

Suited Kings: KQs to K9s (16 hands)

Suited Queens: QJs to QTs (8 hands)

Suited Jacks: JTs (4 hands)

Other Suited: None

Off-Suit Aces: AKo to ATo (48 hands)

Off-Suit Kings: KQo to KTo (36 hands)

Off-Suit Queens: QJo (12 hands)

Off-Suit Jacks: None

Other Off-Suit: None

This distribution includes a total of 200 hands, which is 15 percent (200/1326) of possible starting hands.

As a comparison, the following hands represent a **20-percent distribution**. Hands indicated in bold-faced type are those added to the ones shown in the 15-percent distribution.

Pairs: AA to 77 (48 hands) + **66 (6 hands)**

Suited Aces: AKs to A7s (28 hands) + **A6s to A4s (12 hands)**

Suited Kings: KQs to K9s (16 hands) + **K8s (4 hands)**

Suited Queens: QJs to QTS (8 hands) + **Q9s (4 hands)**

Suited Jacks: JTs (4 hands) + **J9s (4 hands)**

Other Suited: None + **T9s (4 hands)**

Off-Suit Aces: AKo to ATo (48 hands) + **A9o (12 hands)**

Off-Suit Kings: KQo to KTo (36 hands) + **None**

Off-Suit Queens: QJo (12 hands) + **QTo (12 hands)**

Off-Suit Jacks: None + **JTo (12 hands)**

Other Off-Suit: None + **None**

The above distribution includes a total of 200 hands (the 15-percent distribution), plus 70 additional hands, totaling 20.4 percent (270/1326) of possible starting hands. Notice that each hand added (except for 66) includes an 8, 9, Ten, or Ace.

As the final step in the analysis, we can bump the number of includable starting hand combinations up to a **30-percent distribution** (once again added hands are shown in bold):

Pairs: AA to 77 (48 hands) + 66 (6 hands) + **55 (6 hands)**

Suited Aces: AKs to A7s (28 hands) + A6s to A4s (12 hands) + **A3s +A2s (8 hands)**

Suited Kings: KQs to K9s (16 hands) + K8s (4 hands) + **K7s to K5s (12 hands)**

Suited Queens: QJs to QTS (8 hands) + Q9s (4 hands) + **Q8s to Q7s (8 hands)**

Suited Jacks: JTs (4 hands) + J9s (4 hands) + **J8s (4 hands)**

Other Suited: None + T9s (4 hands) + **T8s + 98s (8 hands)**

Off-Suit Aces: AKo to ATo (48 hands) + A9o (12 hands) + **A8o + A7o + A5o (36 hands)** [Not A6o, however.]

Off-Suit Kings: KQo to KTo (36 hands) + None + **K9o (12 hands)**

Off-Suit Queens: QJo (12 hands) + QTo (12 hands) + **Q9o (12 hands)**

Off-Suit Jacks: None + JTo (12 hands) + **J9o (12 hands)**

Other Off-Suit: None + None + **T9o (12 Hands)**

The 30-percent distribution contains a total of 400 hands, which is 30.2 percent (400/1326) of all possible starting hands. Notice again that the majority of hands added to expand starting possibilities beyond the 20-percent and the 15-percent distributions included an 8, 9, Ten, or Ace.

Key Implications of Players Starting-Hand Distributions

The differences among starting-hand distributions as they relate to the expected value of any two cards in your hand is generally not highly relevant for making decisions at the time of the flop. Select a distribution that you feel represents most of the players you will face and memorize it. You will be right most of the time. For actual distributions used that are in the "reasonable" range (which we are defining as 25 to 35 percent of possible starting hands), we feel *you can readily assume everyone uses the same distribution* and you won't be far enough off the mark to incur significant downside risk.

Using the 30-percent distribution we created above as a baseline distribution for opposing players' hands, we can draw some interesting conclusions about what they might be holding when they see a flop:

1. Other players seeing the flop with you will be holding the following cards as the *high card or high combination* in their hands:

Pairs:	15.0 percent (60 hands, all greater than 55)
Ace:	36.0 percent (144 hands, over 50 percent of which have a Ten or greater as a second card)
King:	20.0 percent (80 hands)
Queen:	14.0 percent (56 hands)
Jack or less:	15.0 percent (60 hands)

2. Other players seeing the flop with you will be holding *at least one* of the following cards in their hands:

Ace:	37.5 percent (150 hands)
King:	25.5 percent (102 hands)
Queen:	23.5 percent (94 hands)
Jack:	22.5 percent (90 hands)

Ten:	22.5 percent (90 hands)
Nine:	22.5 percent (90 hands)
Eight:	10.5 percent (42 hands)
Seven:	7.5 percent (30 hands)
Six:	2.5 percent (10 hands)
Five:	5.5 percent (22 hands)
Four:	1.0 percent (4 hands)
Three:	1.0 percent (4 hands)
Two:	1.0 percent (4 hands)

Notice it is about equally likely that another player will be holding a K, Q, J, T, or 9. Aces predominate the holdings with almost 40 percent. If three people see the flop, including you, and you do not hold an Ace, there is only about a one-third chance that you are *not* facing an Ace in at least one of the other two hands.

3. Other players seeing the flop with you will be holding *suited cards* 31.0 percent of the time and *off-suit cards* (including pairs) 69.0 percent of the time.

Distributions for Second and Subsequent Players Entering Pot

Based on our analysis and experience, second and subsequent players entering the pot have somewhat (but not necessarily a whole lot) tighter distributions of possible hands than the initial player to enter. (We are all taught the principle that you need a stronger hand to call or raise a bet than to open the pot first from day one of Hold 'em 101.) We feel that you are safe in assuming that players acting after the first bettor enters the pot are holding ranked pairs or two ranked cards. (If there are three or more players calling or raising before the flop, one (or more) of them likely has a high pair (Aces, Kings, Queens, etc.), AK, or AQ.

A ranked card is a Nine or better.

In Chapter 13, we will use the above analysis combined with a unique method for categorizing flops to create a way of evaluating flops and determining precisely what kinds of hands you are up against. We can then develop effective betting strategies relative to the strength and expectation of our holdings.

13

Evaluating the Flop

II. Reading the Board, Counting Outs, and Computing Pot Odds

IN THIS CHAPTER, we develop a method for analyzing flops and then use that method in Chapter 14 to estimate the relative strength of our holdings versus our read of opponents' holdings. The term P-I-C-K 'R is an easy way to remember the five characteristics associated with categories found on flop boards.

···
The five characteristics represented by the term P-I-C-K 'R are:
  Paired Board
  Su**I**ted Board
  Combo Board
  Ran**K**ed Board
  Rags Board
···

P-I-C-K 'R

The mnemonic P-I-C-K 'R allows us to place each flop board into a specific descriptive category so we can effectively compare those that have similar characteristics against each other. The flop analysis methodology we will develop here differs markedly from methods used by other authors to describe flops. Hence, we begin the discussion by defining each term in our mnemonic.

PAIRED BOARD

A *paired board* occurs when any two cards that you hold (including your hole cards) have completed a pair. If you are holding a pair in the pocket, no matter what cards come on the flop, the board will be paired (or better, if you improve) in relation to your hand. It is also paired for your opponents' hands, but they will not know it. A hidden holding is the most powerful holding of a particular sort. In contrast, a pair among the community cards on the board is common to all hands in play and, therefore, the weakest possible pair in terms of relative strength. In order to form a full house, however, two of the community cards must complete at least a pair. (A full house can also happen when three of a kind appear among community cards.)

The pair is a basic building block for a series of more powerful hands: two pair, three of a kind, full house, and four of a kind. Hence, a hand needs to contain at least a pair if it is to advance to a more powerful combination. Once you have completed a pair in your hand, you have a made hand which will beat any high-card-only hand.

SUITED BOARD

A *suited board* occurs when two or more cards of the same suit appear among the community cards. When a suited board is present, the possibility of a flush or *flush draw* is created if you, or one (or more) of the other players in the hand, are holding cards of that same suit in the pocket.

 A "flush draw" is four cards of the same suit. Another card of that suit must be drawn in order to complete the flush.

COMBO BOARD

A *combo board* occurs when two or more community cards (but not 24, 25, or 35) are separated by no more than two gaps in total. The commonly used terminology for closely grouped cards is *connectors*. A combo board, then, contains some type of connector. Connectors can be one of three types:

Neighbors (two adjacent cards like 89 or KQ)

One-gap connectors (79 or KJ)

Two-gap connectors (69 or KT)

Each connector combination among the community cards represents the possibility that one or more players in the hand is holding a straight or *straight draw*.

 A "straight draw" is four cards that when taken together could build to a completed straight with the addition of one more particular card.

In order for a player to complete a straight using the community cards, there must be at least three cards on the board that are separated by no more than two gaps. Examples of possible straight combinations using three cards are:

23(gap, gap)6 [many people play 45(s) regularly, if they can get in for a small bet, so we have included this combo as an example]

7(gap)9(gap)J

AK(gap, gap)T

Since most sets of five community cards contain a possible straight, learning to recognize straight-building combinations is essential to winning Hold 'em play.

RANKED BOARD

A *ranked board* occurs when the community cards flopped contain one or more cards with a rank of 9 or higher. Recall for a moment our analysis of starting hands for the 30-percent distribution from Chapter 12. The greater majority (about 75 percent) of two-card combinations which will be held by players entering a pot using the 30-percent distribution decision criteria will contain a 9 or higher. If a 9 or higher appears among the community cards, it is very likely that the board has paired someone's pocket cards, or that one or more players have other potentially valuable combos (because they will be holding cards close in rank). For example, if a player holds QJ, and a 9 comes, he now has three to a straight (QJ[gap]9[gap]); this is not a great hand, given, but a slight improvement in terms of winning possibilities over his pocket cards at this point.

RAGS BOARD

A *rags board* occurs when there are no cards higher than an 8 among the community cards, no paired cards, no two same-suited cards (that is, three community cards of different suits—also called a *rainbow flop*), and no combo cards.

Before we can explore the board reading examples in Chapter 14, there are two more subjects we need to introduce: first, a method for counting and estimating the value of *outs;* and second, using pot odds and implied odds to make betting decisions.

Counting "Outs"

An "out" in poker is simply a card that can improve the value of your hand. For example, you hold JT in the pocket, the flop comes 389. At this point you have four consecutive cards (89TJ), which would form a completed straight with the addition of one of two specific cards (7 or Q). This kind of draw is called an *open-ended straight draw.* Since there are four 7s and four Qs in the deck, you have eight *outs* to complete your hand. An open-ended straight draw is a very common situation in Hold 'em.

Another very common situation is a *flush draw*. Assume you have A(d)Q(d) in the pocket (a semi-strong starting hand). The board comes 4(s)T(d)J(d). With the two diamonds on the board you now have four diamonds, giving you a one card draw to a flush. Any diamond on the turn or the river will give you a five diamonds, a flush. Note also that you have the best possible flush because you hold the A(d) (unless a 7(d), 8(d), and/or 9(d) comes making a potential straight flush.) The best possible hand in poker, given the cards on the board, is called the nuts. With the above flop, you have nine outs to the nut flush, a very strong draw. (And, of course, you also have an inside straight draw with any K and a royal flush draw with the K(d). This is a very big *drawing* hand.)

In order to estimate the value of outs, we will approximate the percent of time that you will get the card you need by the 4&2 rule. If you have outs *on the flop (with two cards to come)*, the 4&2 rule states that you will complete your hand by the river about four times the number of outs expressed as a percent. So using the first example in which there are eight outs drawing to an open-ended straight, you will get a Q or 7 to complete your straight about 32 (4 times 8) percent of the time. If you are counting outs *on the turn (with one card to come)*, then you will have about two times the number of outs expressed as a percent. On the turn, an open-ended straight draw with eight outs will complete a straight about 16 percent of the time. Using the same procedure, a flush draw on the flop has a 36 (4 times 9 outs) percent chance to complete by the river. On the turn, a flush draw has an 18 (2 times 9 outs) percent chance.

 An inside straight draw *is a situation where only one rank of card will complete the straight.*

Look back at the second example above, given the flop (the board is 4(s)T(d)J(d), a suited [two diamonds], ranked [JT], combo [JT] flop using P-I-C-K 'R designations), how many outs do you actually have to win the hand if you are holding A(d)Q(d)? We already know that the flush draw gives nine outs. Notice also there is an inside straight draw if a K falls. In this case, any K will make a straight. Since you have already counted the K(d) as part of your flush draw outs, there are three additional K's in the deck that will make a straight.

In addition to the straight draws, you *might* win the hand if your A or Q pairs, because the A and Q are overcards to the board, giving you an additional three A's and three Qs as *possible* outs. The total number of potential outs for this hand is 9 (flush draw) + 3 (inside straight draw) + 3 (pair Aces draw) + 3 (pair Queens draw) = 18 outs total. Suited, ranked, combo flops like this one can produce situations with a high number of outs. Your opponents will frequently have a large number of apparent outs with a highly coordinated board, so expect vigorous betting.

Should you use 18 outs to estimate your chances of winning the hand? Let's assume you have only one opponent and that he made a standard raise pre-flop (about three times the big blind) from a late middle position (say position 5), which you just called with your A(d)Q(d) in the button position (position 7). When your opponent acts after the flop, he leads out with a bet of about one-half the pot. What does he hold and how does his holding affect your computation of outs?

There are two ranked cards on the board. If your opponent is a reasonable bettor, from late middle position he could easily have raised with AK, AQ, AJ, or even AT, KQ, KJ, KT, and perhaps QJ, AA, KK, or QQ. If he were holding a lower pair (JJ, TT, 99, 88, etc), he should have been tempted to raise more than a standard raise to make the call very expensive and thereby discourage a potential caller. He has also made a bet, more or less, in the possible range of standard continuation bets after the flop. He is probably not afraid of a call or raise here.

The best hand he might hold right now is three Js or three Ts. More likely, he holds a high pair (AA, KK, QQ), or a pair of Js or Ts with a strong kicker. Under any of these cases, the hand he now holds probably beats your current hand. If he holds an AJ, AT, QQ, or QJ, he already has a pair. The A or Q in your hand is counterfeited because, when another A or Q falls on the board, your opponent would make two pair or three of a kind, beating your made pair of A's or Q's.

Under these circumstances, the outs associated with the A and Q in your hand should be discounted. Rather than 18 outs, you probably have 12 to 15 solid outs (nine flush draw cards and three Ks), for a minimum 48 (4 times 12) percent chance of completing the hand by the river. Notice that if a K comes on the board, and if your opponent is holding AK, KK, KQ, KJ, or KT, he will be beaten because you would complete at least a straight. Clearly, however, with the holdings and flop discussed, you need to hit one of your outs to have any real confidence you can take the pot, so bet accordingly.

Using Pot Odds and Expected Value

Pot odds are simply the relationship between the amount currently in the pot and the amount you need to bet or invest in the pot in order to win. For example, suppose there is $500 in the pot and you need to invest $100 in order to call and remain in the pot. What are the pot odds? The calculation is done by dividing the current pot by the current bet, or $500/$100. The pot odds are 5 to 1.

Expected value of the pot is the probability you will win the pot multiplied by the amount you will win. If you are currently looking at the flop with a flush draw (9 outs) and two cards to come, your probability of winning given the "4&2 rule" is 36 (4 times 9) percent. (Remember, the 4&2 is an approximation. But it is close enough for any calculation you might need in the midst of a hand.) The expected value of the hand, if there is $500 in the pot, is $500 × 0.36 = $180. On the average, you should win about $180 if you stay in this pot.

Compare expected value to the size of the bet required to win to determine whether the bet is a good investment. Suppose you will need to bet $100 at this time to stay in the hand, is $100 a good bet? If you consider only the bet to be made right now, yes, because the expected value is $180, while the bet, or investment, is $100, yielding a net positive value of $80 *on the average.*

The problem with routinely using expected values for betting decisions in Hold 'em hands, or for that matter in any situation where dynamic interaction occurs, is that the values of probabilities, investments, and payouts are continuously changing over time.

EVALUATING THE FLOP: II. READING THE BOARD ♠ 135

What may have been a great decision with high expected values at one phase of a project may turn out to be a real lemon at a later stage because the shifting dynamics of the situation have altered the underlying decision variables.

No Limit Hold 'em tournament play (which, in our opinion, is a fairly good surrogate for playing conditions encountered over the long-run in real life interpersonal competition) highlights the challenge of using a single static measure, like expected value, to make decisions. For example, you are holding A(h)T(h) with a chip stack of $2000, the pot is $2000, the flop comes J(s)4(h)Q(h). You have the nut flush draw, with an A overcard resulting in 12 fairly good outs (nine hearts and three aces). Your opponent bets $1000. The pot odds your opponent is giving you are ($2000 + $1000)/$1000, or three to one. You expect to win the pot around 50 percent of the time (4&2 rule: 4 times 12 = 48 percent), so the bet is giving you a tremendous edge.

Except for one thing. If you call the $1000 bet, you most likely will need to bet the remainder of your stack on the turn. Given your short stack already, there is almost no way to avoid being all-in by the end of this hand. From an expected value point of view, even with all your chips in, you are getting good odds. But from a tournament survival point of view, you will be out of the tournament 50 percent of the time. Tournaments, unlike cash games, create all or nothing situations that cannot be analyzed using only expected values. In the short-run, you should always call the $1000 bet because it creates value for you. But, the decision has long-term implications for your tournament life.

Situations requiring choices between short-term gain and long-term loss occur frequently in interpersonal competition. For example, the "database" world in which we now live requires constant awareness of how much information is being collected about us and how that information can be used as ammunition against us in interpersonal conflicts. You may, for instance, need to take a small monetary loss in the present in order to avoid having something even remotely negative placed in your credit files. The most innocent of situations, taken out of context, can create havoc because people who have access to your records cannot see all the facts (or choose to ignore, bend or distort them for their own purposes) surrounding what has occurred. Before you take an action with far-reaching implications, step back a moment to consider your alternatives with an eye toward future survival rather than immediate gain.

We will complete our discussion of analyzing flops in Chapter 14 by presenting a number of example hands and flops for analysis. By the end of Chapter 14, you should be familiar with the thought process used to evaluate hands. Further, you should be fairly confident about estimating the range of hands held by opponents based on betting patterns and other indicators.

14

Evaluating the Flop

III. Playing Decisions

MUCH HAS BEEN written over the last few years about multilevel thinking in Hold 'em. As a surrogate for the complexities of multi-level thinking ("I know that you know what I know that you know," or something like that), we feel that every Hold 'em hand should be run through a quick four-step decision-action process, if the hand is to be played at all. (If you intend to fold the hand, of course, go back to chatting with your neighbor.) The mnemonic for the four-step decision-action process is S-K-W-R (pronounced like "skewer").

··

The four steps represented by the mnemonic S-K-W-R are:

Study the Flop

Know Starting Distributions

Wish and Want

Represent the Hand

··

1. Study the Flop. The first and most critical step is to determine what you are holding after the flop. This also turns out to be the easiest and most intuitive step. We believe that you will very quickly become adept at reading your own hand (in self-defense, if for no other reason).

2. Know Starting Distributions. The second step is to determine a range of hands that you believe your opponent might be holding. We strongly advocate your memorizing a starting hand distribution (even if it is just your own). Making an assumption that others at the table are using the same or very similar distributions is a great starting point. If you know something more about your opponents' propensities, then make an adjustment. But without opponent specific information, we feel it is best to make some kind of firm estimate using commonly encountered starting distributions and then use the estimate to project hand ranges.

3. Wish and Want. The third step is to ask yourself what I want my opponents to believe I hold. Most people, in our experience, never take this step. They are perfectly content to look at their own holding, take a stab at figuring out an opponent's holding, and make a bet. When you do not consider what you might want an opponent to think you have, versus simply betting your hand as it stands, you lose the opportunity to manipulate him into betting more than he should or laying down a good hand as a result of a bluff. Manipulating opponents' thinking is the real art of No Limit Hold 'em, and by extension, the real art of succeeding in interpersonal competition.

For every tactic employed, there is another tactic which can defeat it. If your opponents know what you are planning, they can threaten or even defeat you. This is the second principle of interpersonal competition, as we noted in Chapter 1. (The first principle is that everyone is playing the game all the time, so keep your eyes open and your options available.) To defeat a tactic, however, the tactic must be known or at least suspected. By playing Hold 'em in a predictable manner, your tactics become readable and, therefore, useful to smart opponents for the purpose of defeating you. If you are willing to consider throwing in one or two false signals, even if infrequently, you will seriously diminish your opponents' ability to track and defeat what you are doing.

So, to reiterate, the third step in the decision-action process is to decide what you want your opponents to think you have.

4. Represent the Hand. Once you have an idea of the hand you want to represent, the fourth step is to bet your hand in a way that is consistent with what you want your opponent to think. Bet the hand *you are representing* in a straightforward manner (in other words, be obvious about what you are trying to signal).

Attempts to be clever in Hold 'em, or in interpersonal competition for that matter, are generally a waste of time. Why? Most people are too busily involved in their own lives, or hands, to pay sufficient attention to what you are doing. Communication only works when the receiver hears and understands the message. Make the message very simple. I am making a big bet; therefore, I have a big hand. Most people, even bad poker players, understand this message.

For the remainder of this chapter we are going to take four different starting hands and look into ideas of how to play these hands given various kinds of flops under various sets of limiting assumptions. There are obviously millions of possible combinations of pocket cards, flops, assumptions, and responses. Hence, we will only cover the very smallest fraction of the potential discussion. These examples, however, will give you the flavor of how you should handle the four-step decision-action process mentioned above.

Each of the hands we have chosen is problematic to an extent, so you must qualify our comments based on the situation you find yourself in and your own hard-won wisdom. Further, we may not be thinking of everything in our analyses. Our objective is to cover a wide enough range of situations in order to provide an introduction to how you *might* reason through the particular hand/flop combination.

Playing JJ

Paired Jacks create difficulties because the hand is so easily dominated by hands that are frequently played—for example, any hand containing an A, K, or Q, alone or in combination. When the flop comes, there is a fairly good chance (about 50 percent) that an overcard will hit the board. With an overcard, JJ cannot be played strongly for fear of being swamped; but JJ should not be played weakly pre-flop because it is so strong in a showdown.

HAND: J(H)J(S); FLOP: 3(D)8(C)K(S)

According to P-I-C-K 'R, the flop is a ranked, paired (because you hold a pair of jacks) flop, with no pair on board, no suit, no combo. Holding JJ, the only concern would be the K. It is slightly less likely that another person is holding a K than, for example, an A. If there were no significant betting pre-flop (something like your raising to 3 times the big blind and getting a couple of callers), you might want to represent a big pair (which you have) by making a nice continuation bet. Hopefully, everybody else missed and they will fold. A raise could indicate a strong hand, like trips, or maybe a bluff. More troublesome would be a straight call. It might be wise to check and call down the hand if challenged to prevent being trapped for a big loss by someone holding a weak K (say, KT).

HAND: J(H)J(S); FLOP: J(D)7(D)4(S)

This is a ranked, suited (possible flush draws), paired flop, no pair on board, no combo. You have flopped trips, which is a strong hand. The board contains a flush draw, which is dangerous to you. If you slow-play this hand, you are asking for a bad beat. Bet enough so the flush draws do not have odds to call, say 1.5 times the pot, thereby representing a strong hand.

Our experience has shown that betting exactly 1 times the pot, even though the amount does not provide odds for a flush draw (a pot size bet gives the caller 2 to 1 odds; a flush draw theoretically needs more than 2 to 1 for a call), the pot-sized bet will not deter most other players from calling (the "close enough" theory of *losing* poker); therefore, it is better to make the bet more than required. If you get a call here, it is likely a draw or a lesser holding than yours; punish the caller on the turn if a diamond does not fall.

HAND: J(H)J(S); FLOP: T(H)T(S)9(H)

This is a paired, suited, ranked, combo board. Boards do not get much more coordinated than this one. You have two pair with a hidden overpair and two additional backdoor draws (heart flush and multiple straights); even so, you have little chance for improvement. Against you are many possible strong hands and great draws to flushes and straights that will beat your two pair, including the possibility that someone else already holds an overpair to your JJ. Even though you may have the best hand right now, be careful about betting strongly. A check and call strategy might be prudent until you get more information. Be ready to lay the hand down.

HAND: J(H)J(S); FLOP: A(D)J(C)5(S)

The board is ranked, paired, no pair on board (you have trips), no suit, no combo (although a Q or T on turn or river would be a scare card because some [poorer] players would not fold high straight draws with this board because the Broadway straight is probably the nuts). This is a trapping flop for you. If one of your opponents is holding an Ax—particularly A5, or less likely, AJ—she may play it for all she has if she reads you for a strong A or a something like KJ, giving you second pair with adequate kicker.

 Ax = an Ace with any other card.

Represent this hand as an A with a strong kicker (you will probably have bet pre-flop consistent with representing this idea) or small two pair, and you could end up with a big pot against someone who bets small Ax and has hit two pair, or actually has A with strong kicker. Be aware and sensitive that players who have flopped top pair with the A will be reluctant to lay this hand down if bets are reasonable. So keep them reasonable. Show a little weakness, but not so much as to be suspect. Play like a donkey with the second best hand, who does not realize it, and you may actually catch a big pot.

Playing KQ(o)

KQ(o), or off-suited, is difficult to play because it can be dominated by so many hands that opponents would be willing to bet. In order to be comfortable with KQ(o), you *must* (read our lips: "must") get a favorable flop. If you do not get a flop that helps you, be prepared to drop the hand before getting too much invested in what is likely to be a losing proposition.

HAND: K(H)Q(C); FLOP: 3(D)8(C)K(S)

You have flopped top pair with good kicker; a strong flop. When you flop top pair with good kicker, you can easily overplay the hand. Remember that a single pair, even Ks, is not so strong that it can be played like the nuts. In the case of this flop, you can have a relatively high level of confidence that you have the best hand, absent evidence to the contrary. If you are facing one other player, bet aggressively to feel out your opponent. If he plays back at you strongly, but did not raise before the flop, he may have an A, but no pair or a K with a weak kicker. If he just calls, be aware that he may be trapping with trips or two pair (especially if he is the big blind.) If you have more than one opponent, you have a much higher probably that someone holding rags has hit a flop on you. Play softly and be happy to win the hand.

HAND: K(H)Q(C); FLOP: J(D)7(D)4(S)

You have missed entirely. The only play here is check and/or fold. Two overcards are a risky bet unless you have some notion that everyone else has missed the flop and no A is present. Two overcards is a six out situation, or about 24 percent with two cards to come. The pot must give you 3 to 1 odds in order to call a bet. If another player bets pot-size or larger, you do not have the odds to call. The backdoor straight draw you have is worthless for practical purposes.

HAND: K(H)Q(C); FLOP: T(H)J(S)9(H)

You have flopped the nut straight with a backdoor flush draw. If you bet this hand aggressively, everyone will fold to you. As a result, you probably need to let another player catch up with a good "second-best"' hand. If a Q comes, you may end up splitting the pot because so many players would be holding cards in this range. If the board pairs, and someone was calling or raising, be aware that a full house is more likely with this board than many others.

HAND: K(H)Q(C); FLOP: Q(H)8(H)4(H)

You have the second nut flush draw. Since you have four hearts already, there are nine left to complete the flush. The best card that could fall would be A(h). We have seen this type hand lose big many times because players will hold Ax suited quite frequently. Again, play cautiously.

The KQ(o) is a tough hand to play and a tough hand to win with. We recommend that you play the hand carefully, always considering the possibility that someone has you dominated, especially if you pair your Q.

Playing 78(s)

Suited connectors are playable in situations where you can get into the hand fairly cheaply, with several other players betting to raise the pot odds. Suited connectors almost always require judgment after the flop because you will have overcards on the board. If you cannot make a premium hand with your connectors (usually a flush playing both cards), then it is best to fold right away. A single pair with one of the cards is extremely vulnerable and not likely a winner. One more comment: We have noted a trend in tournament play for players with a short stack to go all-in when they hold 78(s).

HAND: 7(S)8(S); FLOP: 3(S)8(C)K(S)

You have flopped middle pair with a flush draw. With mid-range suited connectors, you will seldom, if ever, have the nut flush draw. Most of the time, however, when you are using both pocket cards to complete a flush (that is, there are only three suited cards on the board), you can be reasonably confident (maybe 80 percent) you have the best hand. This is a fairly strong drawing hand, with about ten outs to win the hand (nine spades plus two eights less one for the times you lose to a bigger flush; you might also be willing to count three 7s, which give you two pair, as one [not three] additional out). On the flop, with two cards to come, you have at least a 40 percent chance of hitting a winner, so the hand can be played strongly for the turn card because you will certainly have pot odds.

HAND: 7(S)8(S); FLOP: J(D)7(D)4(S)

You have flopped middle pair with no draws except the two 7s. This is a losing situation and needs to be folded unless there is very little betting.

HAND: 7(S)8(S); FLOP: T(H)J(S)9(H)

You have flopped bottom straight with a backdoor flush draw. The bottom-end straight is highly suspect, but still a good hand. The cards that follow will determine whether you need to be concerned about another higher straight beating you. In this situation, you may want to bet strongly on the flop, if you are not already heads-up, to limit the field. Remember that the KQ represents the other end of the straight. KQ is a hand that a lot of players will not throw away pre-flop under any circumstances, but particularly when faced with only a small bet to stay in the pot, so be prepared to lay down your straight if someone plays back at you strongly.

HAND: 7(S)8(S); FLOP: Q(H)8(H)4(H)

Whenever three suited cards flop, unless you hold one (A or K) or two of that suit yourself, your hand is reasonably weak. Players will stick with the hand if they have any high suited card, so you will not get them out by betting. We generally will fold this hand quickly rather than try to push others out.

Suited connectors are an excellent type of hand to broaden your starting hand range. They do well against high pairs because if you hit your cards, you will generally have a strong enough hand to beat a lone pair, two pair, or trips. Suited connectors will not win most of the time, so you need to make the most of it when you get a favorable flop.

Playing AK(o)

Because AK(o), or "Big Slick," is such a powerful hand, many players are reluctant to lay it down and will overplay the hand. We have seen a few players who will not lay it down in any situation until they have seen the river card. Falling in love with AK is a mistake. Any pair will beat this combination, if neither A nor K falls on the board. Before the flop, you have only a 50-percent chance you will pair one of the cards by the river. After the flop, you have a 24-percent chance.

HAND: A(S)K(D); FLOP: 3(S)8(C)K(S)

This type of flop is very strong when holding AK. There is an above average chance that you currently hold the best hand. The problem here is overconfidence. You can be trapped easily, so watch how others bet. Always keep in mind that top pair with a strong kicker is a good hand, but it is definitely not a hand to be played recklessly. If a clever opponent has flopped two pair or trips, he will be hoping you have AK so he can trap you. Bet carefully and pay attention to the actions of others.

HAND: A(S)K(D); FLOP: J(D)7(D)4(S)

You have a busted flop and a weak overall hand. Although you might still have the best hand, anyone playing with you will have a made hand or a draw that will beat your unpaired AK. Lay the hand down in the face of a confident bet.

HAND: A(S)K(D); FLOP: T(H)J(S)Q(H)

Flopping a Broadway straight is a dream hand except for the fact you may not make any money with it. If you have bet aggressively before the flop, your opponents will suspect (correctly) you now have a strong hand. They will flee when you bet. Take a moment to think about how you might convince your opponents that you are on a draw, or a busted hand of some sort which you are trying to bluff.

The art of making real money at Hold 'em is using your opponents' false conceptions of reality against them. If you can, bet in such a way that it appears you are hesitant or confused or afraid (make your hand tremble, it's a tell that everyone knows, but not everyone will be fooled either). Rather than just bet out, try something else. It might work.

HAND: A(S)K(D); FLOP: Q(D)8(D)4(D)

Three diamonds on the flop plus the K(d) in your hand makes this a strong flop. If the betting before the flop has been frisky, however, you may well be facing the A(d), so take care. We would not try to maximize the bets here, but rather keep the pot reasonable because the chances of someone staying in the hand without a strong diamond is small.

Adopting Orphans

An orphan flop is one that consists of cards that are unlikely to have been matched by cards played pre-flop. A rags board like 8(s)4(d)2(h), or a paired, unranked board like 7(s)7(d)2(h) (our favorite), should be adopted if possible. You get this chance most often in the small blind or big blind. If you bet out from the small or big blind when rags show up (thereby adopting the orphan board), there is a reasonable chance that everyone else will fold. Other players will have raised and called pre-flop with decent hands. These kinds of boards offer no hope of improvement for their relatively strong pre-flop cards. Betting implies you have benefited from a "blind special"; players will often fold rather than take a chance that you have hit a monster hand.

Analyzing flops for potential is a key part of winning at Hold 'em. Using our four-step decision-action process (S-K-W-R), you can focus in on those aspects of the hand that give you an opportunity to profit. To reiterate the process:

1. Determine what you hold after the flop in terms of composition and relative strength. (Study the flop.)

2. From pre-flop betting and assumed hand ranges, predict the range of hands your opponents might be holding and how strong they are. (Know starting distributions.)

3. Determine what you want your opponents to believe you hold. (Wish and want.)

4. Bet your hand in a way that represents the hand you want your opponents to put you on. (Represent the hand.)

Using the four-step decision-action process, you will be able to occasionally (but certainly not always) deceive your opponents about the strength of your hand. If you consistently keep yourself alert to being trapped or self-deluded, you stand a good chance of effectively improving your poker profits over the long run.

15

The SWORD in Hand

Tactics I

FROM THE EARLIEST days after we are born, we create, test, evaluate, refine, and practice tactics in order to fulfill our needs. Young children are masters of the art of tactical adaptation, maneuver, and execution. Adults are also fairly adept at using tactics (having been children themselves once), but the need to simplify, condense, and organize the highly complex and sophisticated world in which they must function often causes a reduction in flexibility and ingenuity with respect to creating and employing tactics. We depend a great deal on previously developed models of behavior and previously acquired assumptions about ourselves and others. As a result, we tend to limit our choices in tactics to fewer, more predictable, behaviors that *seemed* to have work for us as we progress through our lives.

As we have pointed out in previous chapters, these models, while effective at reducing *apparent* complexity and decreasing the *apparent* number of decision variables, tend to limit our vision and predetermine our actions under certain conditions, particularly actions taken in ordinary, everyday situations. Astute observers (especially astute poker players) can and do utilize our predictability to model our behavior. Virtually everyone moves in patterns that change little from day to day, except over long periods of time. Hence, our thinking methods can be classified and defeated(!) rather easily. (Remember our earlier advice to live as if someone is watching you at all times. Someone is.)

Interpersonal competition is seldom physical in our world. Battles among individuals and organizations take the form of pitting one line of tactical thinking and maneuver against another line to determine which prevails, much like poker. Other things being equal (though they never are), the competitor who obtains the clearest vision of the situation that really exists (not the situation he has predetermined exists, or the situation he wants to exist), and who practices the greatest depth of tactical thinking, has the best *opportunity* to achieve victory. There are no guarantees, however, even for the very best players.

Understanding the battlefield tactical situation, evaluating the nature of tactical alternatives that are reasonably available given the situation, and creating an effective mix of actionable tactics in anticipation of, and in response to, those applied by competing individuals and groups are the fundamental steps to success in any competition. This idea is the essence of the concepts taught by Sun Tzu in *The Art of War.*

To enhance our ability to understand and apply tactics to interpersonal competition in general, and to Texas Hold 'em in specific, we turn to another classic Chinese book from the same period of history as *The Art of War.* Titled *The Thirty-Six Stratagems,* this text can be considered a practical addendum to the higher-level strategic advice provided by Sun Tzu. *The Thirty-Six Stratagems* is a short handbook of tactical methods, which can be used as building blocks to develop workable alternatives for tactical action under the stress of competition. (See Appendix C for a summary of *The Thirty-Six Stratagems* used here.)The tactics covered anticipate a wide range of competitive conditions and can be readily applied to many competitive problems, including those encountered in a session of Texas Hold 'em.

Using ideas from *The Thirty-Six Stratagems* as a starting point, we will expand and modernize the original tactical concepts with three goals in mind:

1. Our first goal is to explain what each tactic intends to achieve in simple, practical, executable terms so you can determine whether a particular tactic fits your needs.

2. Our second goal is to evaluate the types of circumstances under which you might use the tactic, or under which you may expect the tactic to be used against you.

3. Our third goal is to consider what kinds of assets (people, money, and other assets) might need to be employed in order to make the tactic work for you, or to defeat the tactic, if it is used against you.

In other words, we will seek to provide clarity of purpose, situational applicability, and essential resources required for each tactic. The keyword for grouping *The Thirty-Six Stratagems* is S-W-O-R-D.

....
The five groups represented by the keyword S-W-O-R-D are:
Strength
Weakness
Opportunity
Replacement
Disguise
....

Sun Tzu said: "The art of war is based on deception." Although some of the tactics in S-W-O-R-D are straightforward, most involve the use of deception or misdirection to leverage an opponent, thereby obtaining the greatest effect at the lowest cost and risk.

Success in competition depends upon carefully thinking through competitive situations using whatever time you have available. Sun Tzu said: "The competitor who thinks the most before entering the battle will win." Take a moment to review the keyword N-O-T-E covered in Chapter 6. Think before you act. Rote or habitual application of tactics to situations will result in your defeat. Failing to anticipate how your opponent may react to your movements will allow him to surprise or deceive you.

Tactics cannot be executed in a vacuum. The probability of success for each tactic depends in part upon tactics utilized in previous situations and the anticipation of tactics to be employed later. A tactic must be placed into the context of a continuing flow of strategy and fit the overriding character of the competitive approach being applied.

Tactics work when your opponent reacts in a manner you expect. For the appropriate reaction to occur, you must understand how your opponent reasons, how he decides. If you are in concert with your opponents' reasoning processes, you can orchestrate and exploit his responses. This is the goal. Tactics are not ends in themselves, but the means by which we maneuver opponents into defeat.

Tactics Based on Strength

Tactics based on strength require you to execute actions without incurring the undue risk that counterattacks or enemy maneuvers can cripple or harm you significantly. You must have enough localized power to protect yourself. But even when your opponent is unable to threaten you by force, he remains smart and crafty and dangerous, so carefully apply some of the following tactics to deal with the situation. The specific combination of tactics you choose will depend upon your specific goals:

♦ *Beat the grass to startle the snakes* **(Snake in the Grass Tactic).** Snakes hide themselves in the grass until they sense an opportune moment to strike. If you intend to move through the grass, find out where the snakes are hiding first. The key to this tactic is to create a startling event. It can be anything that will cause hidden opponents to react so you can identify and locate them.

In Hold 'em, an unexpected raise (on your part) can sometimes cause a player trying to trap you to reveal the strength of his hand too quickly by reraising. Any bet or move that creates a sense of uncertainty in Hold 'em will throw an opponent off balance.

Sometimes comments or tells that are choreographed properly can startle others.

♦ *Use a loan to rob the bank* (**Other Peoples' Money Tactic**). If you are faced with multiple opponents, it may be possible to form a partnership with one or more of them in which the partners are willing to lend you some resources to defeat a common foe. Take these loaned resources and then use them to defeat all your opponents, even those who lent them. Stealing blinds in the middle rounds of a No Limit Hold 'em tournament can build up your stack so you are able to push your opponents in later rounds.

♦ *Remove the head and the body falls* (**Guillotine Tactic**). Many groups are bound together by a single strong leader. If you are able to defeat the leader, the entire group will fall. Identify the person who provides the drive and vision for a group whose ideas you oppose. Knock him off course. This will demotivate his followers and render them harmless as a group force. If there is one stronger player at the table who is able to counter your moves effectively, look for the chance to take him out. Weaker players will then lose heart and you can dominate play.

♦ *Fight a tired enemy* (**Play Hide and Seek Tactic**). Fatigue weakens both body and mind. Whenever you can, create situations where your opponent must work very hard while you are able to take it easy. A tired opponent makes mistakes more readily than a fresh one. Encourage your opponent to chase around after red herrings and straw dogs. Rest while he pursues shadows. When you are able to control the time and place of an engagement, you have a distinct advantage. Bring the enemy to you and tire him out on the way. Many players will sit at the poker table even after they have lost the ability for sharp thinking through fatigue or alcohol consumption. Take full advantage of a weary, impaired, or distracted opponent. Encourage people to overdo their intake of alcohol or to stay at the table when they are tired or tilted.

♦ *If the head is protected, attack the feet* (**Achilles Heel Tactic**). Attacking a well-protected or well-financed foe can be dangerous and expensive. It is often easier to aim for some aspect of his program that is valuable to him, but not as well guarded. No opponent can defend every point on his battle line without stretching his resources too thin. If the point you wish to attack is too heavily shielded, look for a point of vulnerability that has been neglected. Your opponent will be forced to redeploy his forces to defend a place that is under pressure from a stronger force. This will throw him off balance. Every poker player has certain weaknesses in his game. If you try to beat someone where he is best, you may drain your own resources and energy. Look for the point of weakness and focus your energy there.

♦ *Desperate people fight to the death* (**False Hope Tactic**). An opponent with his back up against a wall and no way to escape will fight harder because he has nothing to lose, and he fears death. Always give your opponents the perception that there is a way for them to escape the trap. When a trapped antagonist sees a possible way out, he will focus his energies on getting away rather than fighting you. If his escape route is nothing more than a dead end, it may be easier to capture him when he finds out.

Sometimes it is difficult to get a stubborn player to push his chips into the pot. He will hang on, hand after hand, always a threat to come back. If the opportunity presents itself, give him an apparent way to make himself stronger and trap him into a bad bet or two. These mistakes and loses may discourage him enough that he gives up and surrenders his chips without so vigorous a fight.

♦ *Confusion catches fish* (**Rattle the Cage Tactic**). Always be alert for the chance to create confusion. As we have noted earlier, unmanaged predictability is a severe weakness. The less confident your opponent is about what you are trying to accomplish, the more latitude you have to be creative and forceful with your moves. When you are planning some type of action, develop a way to muddy the waters around your movements so observers will not be quite sure about what you are doing. The more they must guess, the weaker their response to your approach. A confused fish might just swim right into your net.

In Hold 'em, confusing your opponents is probably the strongest weapon available to you. Make every attempt to throw them off track by playing hands in a manner that suggests something other than what you have. The whole point of our four-step decision-action process in evaluating flops (S-K-W-R, see Chapter 14) and the key-word R-A-P-T (see Chapter 6) is to have you think about what hand you might represent in order to sow a little confusion, rather than just betting the hand you actually hold in a straightforward way. If you can fool the table once or twice, they will be scratching their heads all the time and perhaps handing over their chips too.

Tactics Based on Weakness

Relative weakness (even if only perceived) is a much more common state than relative strength, both in Hold 'em and in interpersonal competition. The tactics described in the following section are designed to be used either when you are weaker than your opponent or your opponent is known to be weaker than you are, but he cannot be approached directly:

♦ *Lure a tiger from his stronghold* (**Big Cat Tactic**). When facing a tiger, we need every advantage we can get because we will be the weaker party. A tiger is simply more powerful and more capable than we are in his natural setting. A tiger that is familiar with and protected by his surroundings and environment is often too formidable a foe to defeat. To fight a tiger, we must induce him out of his fortress, pull him out of his comfort zone. Essentially, we must put the tiger on tilt, so we can outmaneuver him at a place and time in which we can establish some kind of local advantage (numbers or terrain or finances, etc.)

Getting a tiger to leave the safety of his home territory requires baiting him in some fashion. The more clever the tiger, the stronger and more appealing the bait must be. Further, a tiger will become suspicious quite quickly. Your plans and execution must be flawless and virtually undetectable.

Often, in Hold 'em, you must be the recipient of a substantial serving of good fortune to beat a tiger when he is in his element and on his game. Distracting or tilting him will require a cool head and a perceptive, creative approach. He will know how to defend himself against anything ordinary.

♦ *Keep strong friends over there and weak enemies close by* **(Weak Neighbor Tactic).** Friends are problematic, especially those who are more powerful than you are. Allies tend to remain allies only so long as there is some kind of benefit from doing so. When a more lucrative offer comes along, they will turn on you in a heartbeat. A powerful, but friendly, neighbor is a good thing so long as the relationship blooms. One sour note, one profitable alternative, and your neighbor becomes a difficult foe with designs on your territory.

To offset this kind of problem, make friends with strong parties who are somewhat removed from you in distance or interest, while keeping those nearer to you a bit estranged. Strong friends, who can provide ready assistance when you are threatened, tend to keep envious and greedy neighbors at bay. If you decide it is in your interest to attack one of your neighbors, a strong friend at a distance can provide assistance without becoming a threat himself while you are weakened by a fight.

♦ *Arouse darker emotions to further your own schemes* **(Sin, Seduction, and Anger Tactic).** Arousing darker emotions—fear, greed, hate, lust, jealousy, suspicion, anger—can both empower and cloak your ultimate goals. Sowing seeds of discord among enemies using the lure of sex, money, or power can rip apart the strongest foe making him ripe for conquest.

Tactics that arouse darker emotions usually involve the employment of agents and the cooperation of other people. Involving several people in the execution of a tactic always makes secrecy difficult. When you find it necessary to employ agents and to rely on others to execute your plans in secret, you must also be prepared for, and always anticipate, leaks, whether intentional, through spies and double agents, or unintentional, through errors in judgment or weakness in character. Keep a wary eye on your co-conspirators. They will betray you.

Fear and anger are ever present in Hold 'em. Fear allows more aggressive players to push less aggressive players around. Anger pops up all the time (because bad beats and lousy cards are far more common than the more fortunate ones). Even the calmest individual can become highly frustrated when Lady Luck smacks him unfairly a couple of times. Fear and anger are the tools of tilt. Magnify them if you can. Take a look back at the keyword D-I-S-C-A-R-D in Chapter 7. All of the ideas behind the D-I-S-C-A-R-D concept depend on rousing some type of emotion to screen off and deflect another player's better judgment.

♦ *Arouse empathy with self-inflicted losses* **(Poor Puppy Tactic).** When you are faced with a situation in which you will surely lose or be compromised (for example, when you are a hostile agent placed inside the enemy camp), it may be necessary to inflict harm on yourself to arouse the empathy of your opponents or deflect their suspicion. The reasoning goes that people do not normally hurt themselves. If you have been injured or harmed for the apparent benefit of your opponent, the wound serves as de facto evidence that you were fighting on your opponent's behalf. This tactic has been used over and over throughout history with great success because self-sacrifice tends to create huge amounts of empathy. Application can, however, be painful and the level of success eventually depends on whether you can sustain the fabric of your deception over a period of time.

♦ *Hide weakness behind illogical actions* **(Stand Back Tactic).** One of the greatest fears people have is loss of face, even in the generally faceless society of America. Most people are highly embarrassed when they are faked out or bluffed, making them extremely sensitive to signs of inconsistent behavior that would foreshadow some kind of bluffing maneuver or other trickery.

Bluffing is a tactic that should be used infrequently. (Despite widely-held beliefs, bluffing in a real poker game is not as common a practice as people might think, because the risks do not justify the gains in many cases. See more on bluffing in Chapters 19 and 20.)

When we bluff a situation in Hold 'em, by definition we are holding nothing of real value. The other person has us dominated. We are depending upon an opponent's overly active imagination to provide the substance of our victory. It is what he thinks we have that counts, and what he thinks we have will be based completely on his observations of our actions and how those observations fit into his poker experience and training. In Chapter 10, we discussed the keyword P-I-N-G (Pose, Inquire, eNgage, Group) in relation to determining the character-type exhibited by others. Bluffing depends almost entirely on our ability to create and sustain an effective, believable, consistent Pose. When we have established a definite and identifiable pose, we can manipulate the perceptions of our opponents so they become suspicious of our actions and begin to imagine something might be out of place. A well-developed pose is the backdrop against which we are able to enact a bluff based on an opponent's aroused suspicion.

♦ *Know when to run away* **(Hyena Tactic).** There are battles which should not be fought and which cannot be won. Recognizing situations in which we are already defeated because of factors outside our control or influence is critical to longer-term survival. If you are continuously fighting battles you cannot win, you will run out of resources, energy, or time. When you know you are beaten, give it up and get out. Save your time and talent for future battles that are winnable.

The defining difference between good Hold 'em players and great Hold 'em players, particularly in No Limit tournament play, is the ability to lay down a hand when necessary. No Limit tournament play is a marathon rather than a sprint. There are always, it seems, periods of time during which no playable hands arrive. You may sit for an hour or more tossing in hand after hand. All of a sudden you are on the button with A(c)K(c). A middle-position player puts in a big raise. You look at your hand. He has got to be bluffing, right? You raise all-in and he turns over AA. You are dominated and dead in the water. Looking at this hand dispassionately, it is easy to see that, at best, you are going to have a race for all your chips because of the sizable raise from middle position (that is, he probably has a big pair, and as a consequence, about a 55-percent to 45-percent advantage). Unless you must, you do not want to face a coin-flip for all your chips; it is simply too risky. Folding your beautiful AK hand is a better choice considering there will be another hand to play in a moment. A large component of luck is timing. Think the situation through rather than react emotionally. Fight if you have an advantage; run if you do not.

16

The SWORD in Hand

Tactics II

CHAPTER 16 continues the discussion of *The Thirty-Six Stratagems* using the keyword S-W-O-R-D to organize the tactical ideas presented. (See Appendix C for a summary of *The Thirty-Six Stratagems* used here.) In the course of the next few pages, we will cover tactics based on **Opportunity** and **Replacement**. (Tactics based on **Disguise** will be discussed in Chapter 17.)

Tactics based on opportunity are grounded in factors related to conditions occurring at a specific place and time. Opportunistic tactics require, first, an eye for the possibilities inherent in a situation as they may manifest themselves unexpectedly, and second, a bias for taking action on the fly when the chance occurs.

Tactics based on replacement generally involve actions that substitute one item (usually of lesser value) for another item (usually of greater value). Replacement tactics are a kind of strategic sleight of hand that leaves your opponent holding something other than he originally believed he was holding.

Tactics Based on Opportunity

Taking advantage of opportunity allows you to use surprise as a weapon in the process of executing your tactics. Surprise multiplies the impact of tactics and leverages the strength of actions taken. Flexibility of thought and maneuver underlie the success of opportunistic tactics. If you intend to move swiftly and strike suddenly, you will need to prepare yourself through practice and study beforehand.

♦ *Steal a couple of sheep while the shepherd is busy elsewhere* (**Carpe Diem Tactic**). Profit and gain should be realized whenever the chance presents itself. If sheep become scattered and the shepherd is somewhere else chasing down a portion of his flock, do not hesitate to weigh the possibility of collecting one or two animals for yourself, particularly if your role in the action can remain undetected. Be intelligent and careful about applying this tactic. Stealing someone else's sheep, however easily accomplished at times, is still theft and could be quite dangerous, not to mention always illegal. In many other cases, though, especially where ownership of items is not clearly established, there may be ample basis for claiming the items for yourself. Whenever circumstances allow you to profit from the carelessness, laziness, stupidity, or poor luck of others without breaking the law or endangering your health, consider how this might be done.

In tournament Hold 'em, when blinds have increased to a substantial proportion of an average stack, it is always necessary to look for every chance to steal them for yourself. Stealing blinds and antes at least once each round can keep you active in a tournament until you get a playable hand. Stealing blinds and antes also means another player cannot get them, thereby weakening others' positions.

♦ *If you cannot attack your opponent directly, then steal his firewood* (**Short Supply Tactic**). Sometimes an enemy is far too strong to attack openly, but leaves an open avenue to his resources. An opponent may not realize the vulnerability of financial, emotional, or personal resources and, as a consequence, fail to adequately defend them. If you are able to take the firewood from under his cooking pot, he will not be able to eat and become weak, allowing you an advantage.

Whittle away at another player's emotional stability whenever possible. Upsetting another player, even in a small way, can create carelessness or volatility in the play of hands. It can make judgment less precise and mistakes more likely. Every person has a weak spot in his personal armor. Keep tapping on his helmet until he responds with annoyance. It only takes one poorly played hand to eliminate an opponent from a tournament. Maintain your own balance while becoming a pain in the ass to others.

♦ *Lock the doors while the thieves are still inside* **(Locked Door Tactic).** Thieves and other scoundrels are adept at entering areas in order to pilfer your valuables. If you discover a theft in progress, don't chase the thieves outside, but rather lock the doors to trap them inside. By locking the doors, you can capture the thieves and end their looting once and for all. If you allow bandits to escape, they will return again and again.

You will often face other players who are attempting to steal a pot from you. When possible, turn the tables and trap them so they will be reluctant to try it again. Loose, aggressive players can be encouraged to become arrogant and careless if they are allowed to succeed in their overbearing play strategies for a short while. Lay down a few inexpensive hands to loose, aggressive players and they will try to run over you every hand. This tendency will allow you to snap them off eventually. If you maintain your patience, you will get your chance and your payback.

♦ *Watch a firefight from the other side of the river* **(Hands-Off Tactic).** When two or more of your opponents are engaged in a firefight, it is wiser to watch them destroy each other from a safe distance. Allowing opponents to weaken and cripple each other without being able to harm you is an excellent method for gaining an advantage. You should be close enough to the scene to accurately observe the action (so you can enter the battle at an appropriate moment). On the other hand, you should also stay far enough away that your enemies don't decide you are an easy target for their combined forces and attack you before going back to their own mutual destruction.

In tournament Hold 'em play, it is almost always advantageous to eliminate another player. If you can get someone else to take the risk of going all in while you stand by and watch the action, it may work out to your advantage. The best scenario is getting two smaller chip stacks to battle each other. One or the other will double up in the end, but one will go out leaving fewer opponents to deal with.

♦ *Lure your opponent onto the roof before removing his ladder* (**Up a Creek Tactic**). Coat the entrance to a trap with honey. Give opponents an easy and obvious way to get what they want, so they pursue it vigorously without much real thought. Once they have ascended onto the roof (or into the hole), take away their ladder. Greed and lust create blinders on many people. They will throw away caution and ignore their own experience to get at a prize they consider valuable.

Inexperienced poker players will often judge the desirability of entering a hand by counting the chips in the pot without weighing the associated risk. If you are able to pave the way into a pot with gold, a greedy opponent may discount or ignore the risk that you have her beaten, or may overestimate the strength of her hand in her rush to grab the chips. Find a way to confirm her in this folly. The best players trap opponents using their opponents' own desires and assumptions. Figure out what your opponents want and give them the appearance of being able to obtain it—if they will just climb up on the roof. "Here, I'll hold the ladder for you so you won't fall (yet)."

♦ *Loot a burning house* (**Hot Hand Tactic**). The chaos and confusion that accompany unexpected misfortune often open avenues of profit for those who move quickly. When people are distracted by the immediate need to put out a fire, they will not pay as much attention to areas which may have become vulnerable as a result of stress or damage associated with the emergency. Where there is smoke there is profit, for those who are prepared and are willing to act.

Bad beats can cause an intense emotional reaction. A player cannot help but feel cheated when he is beaten by an improbable draw. When the emotional reaction is extreme, be ready to take advantage of any lapse in concentration. Players on tilt are prone to make huge mistakes until they cool off. These mistakes are the gateways to profit.

◆ *Replace solid beams with rotten timbers* (**House of Cards Tactic**). Every successful enterprise depends upon relatively few key players to maintain organizational and cultural integrity. Every skilled person depends upon a few key principles of behavior or proven methods of operation to sustain a continuing high level of accomplishment. If key aspects (solid beams) of success are replaced by ideas of less quality or strength (rotten timbers), the entire fabric of the organization or person is weakened. When you are in competition with others, look for key elements that support and define your opponents' main talents and skills. Test your competitors' belief and trust in these elements. If possible, sow seeds of doubt or confusion to weaken their framework of achievement.

There are a wide range of options for constructing a workable strategy to play Texas Hold 'em at a fairly high level of skill and profit. Once you have learned how to play correctly, selecting those options which are comfortable for you is a matter of preference and temperament. In addition to the wide range of workable strategies available, there are truckloads of plausible sounding, but completely perverse, opinions about what works in Hold 'em.

Become an expounder (but not a practitioner) of bad ideas. A fairly large proportion of Hold 'em players are willing to try almost any kind of garbage idea because someone else mentions it. A few bad suggestions presented knowledgeably at the poker table can do much to derail gullible but otherwise competent players. A possible dividend from the rotten timber strategy is that a few of the more skilled players might think you really are a bad player. But, what the heck, maybe they will actually underestimate you in a critical situation.

Tactics Based on Replacement

Replacement tactics are based on the premise that people use mental models of reality to organize and classify perceptions. When someone sees a familiar object, he will often categorize the object without investigating it more closely. If it walks like a duck, swims like a duck, and quacks like a duck, it probably is a duck (or some such similar reasoning process). Understanding how to apply replacement tactics offers you a selection of relatively subtle maneuvers which can be applied in a variety of circumstances, particularly in the arena of interpersonal competition where direct confrontation may be counterproductive.

♦ *Leave behind a golden shell* **(Shell Game Tactic).** It is sometimes necessary, in the course of business, to preserve our health and welfare by slinking away from the battlefield unnoticed. Often, however, the difficulty with escape is that our absence from the scene is readily apparent and triggers rapid pursuit. To avoid detection, we need to create a shell that will serve as our surrogate and as a focus of attention for the critical moments when we are still close enough to be captured.

One of the more famous examples of the application of the golden shell tactic was accomplished by George Washington after the Second Battle of Trenton in New Jersey. Washington's army was trapped by the British as night fell. The British forces intended to attack the next morning, so they settled in for the night. Instead of sitting around awaiting the morning attack, Washington ordered his army to slip through the British lines in small groups during the night. The façade he used to hide his movements was burning campfires. He left enough men in camp to maintain the campfires as if the entire army were still in residence. When the British arrived the next morning, all they found were burned-out campfires. The men had escaped.

♦ *Turn the guest into the host* **(Grab the Reins Tactic).** The closer you are to your opponents, the more you are likely to learn about their weaknesses and points of vulnerability. A guest in someone else's domain may be able to obtain privileged access to information not available to an outsider. Used effectively, information can create the leverage needed to shift the base of power within the domain. The guest reverses his position and becomes the host. Staging a coup within the walls of an opponent's castle or business is a tricky maneuver. To be successful, the objective of the action cannot suspect he is being targeted. There must be a reasonable screen of trust (which you will eventually betray) that deflects suspicion and reduces vigilance.

At the poker table, a given player may dominate action for a period of time through luck or aggressive play. Watching his actions carefully, you can hope to uncover a weak spot in his strategy. If you can trap him or embarrass him with his own weakness, the deflation of emotion from his loss of dominance can unbalance his game and increase the probability of a major mistake on his part. The role reversal tactic is particularly effective against players who, for some reason or other, have a sense of entitlement—they feel they deserve to win because they are just better people than you (using whatever dimensions of measurement they consider relevant) or anyone else at the table might be.

♦ *Aim right; shoot left* **(Innuendo Tactic).** Sometimes an opponent's position or status makes it impossible to consider direct action against him. In order to criticize, needle, or embarrass a person in this kind of protected position, you may be required to aim at a substitute target. The innuendo tactic is more effective against opponents who are perceptive or sensitive (for whatever reason). It is often said that bluffs do not work against unskilled players. For the same reasons, innuendo does not work against insensitive targets.

Upsetting other players at the table is a fine art when accomplished skillfully. You are, however, almost always constrained from direct verbal abuse as a weapon. Indirect assault using straw men as substitute aiming points is often just as effective in drawing the ire of the selected subject, but less likely to be perceived as falling outside allowable limits of civility by the dealer or floor person.

People are often highly protective of their mistaken judgments; the more stupid the play, the more excuses are needed and often supplied (the most frequent bad excuse being pot odds). If another player makes an error, turn to your neighbor and start talking about a situation you saw on the World Poker Tour. (Or anywhere else. Make it up if needed.) If you get this right, you can have the targeted player absolutely boiling without saying a word about his actual play. If you are lucky, he will eventually create a disturbance at the table.

♦ *Even false flowers look real from a distance* **(False Flower Tactic).** Selling someone a dead tree can be problematic. Not only is the tree, not merely, really, and sincerely dead, but it probably appears to be dead too. The false flower tactic creates the illusion of health and vitality by attaching fake flowers to a dead tree. If the client (or mark, if you prefer) does not investigate the tree closely, she may not notice the ruse. The key to this kind of illusion is creating a comfort zone for the client in which she has little reason to question the reality of the illusion, or in which she overrides her common sense because of greed or lust.

Executing a stone cold bluff in Hold 'em requires that the other player believe you have the kind of hand you do not. Creating a major bluff usually requires a set up. The targeted player must have every reason to believe you are holding the hand you represent. It is necessary that you pay attention to your own betting patterns, even on hands you eventually throw away. Further, be aware of the implications of hands that you show down when it is not required. Every piece of information that you give the table should lead other players to the conclusion you want.

♦ *Breathe life into a corpse (**CPR Tactic**).* Symbols are powerful reference points for attracting attention and usurping power. The purpose of the CPR tactic is to attach yourself to a widely-recognized but somewhat out-of-vogue symbol (this is the corpse). The greater the emotional current surrounding the symbol, the more latent power the symbol contains; and, as a consequence, the more valuable it becomes if you can resurrect the body of the symbol for your own purposes (that is, make it live for you).

Because our minds make extensive use of symbols to represent variables in the mental decision models we create, symbols are shortcuts to arousing and focusing emotion. Politicians, religious leaders, demagogues of every sort, depend on the manipulation of symbols to achieve their purposes, both benign and insidious. If a picture is worth a thousand words, then an effective symbol is worth a million.

♦ *Keep a scapegoat handy (**Scapegoat Tactic**).* Unforeseen difficulties, unexpected blunders, even unavoidable tragedies can raise the specter of failure and attract the all-consuming finger of blame. The negative impact of failure can be muted by using a scapegoat as a shield. The scapegoat is an honored tradition in human affairs (though few scapegoats might consider it so). Rather than accept the consequences of mistakes, society would prefer that some individual or group be unequivocally burdened with the entire fault for whatever event requires atonement. The sacrifice of the few washes away the sins of the many, or so they say.

Sooner or later, if you intend to play in the arena of power, you will find it necessary to employ the scapegoat tactic to cover up your own mistakes, or to avoid being manipulated by others. The essential characteristic of a good scapegoat is the ability to channel and dissipate large amounts of emotional energy quickly and impersonally (like a human lightening rod). To be effective, the scapegoat must plausibly represent some facet of fault, or defect of character, that can be associated with the causes of a specific failure and which can be enlarged upon enough to generate a flash point, a climax. When it occurs, the intensity of the flash point should shock emotions and cauterize wounds so a society or group can realize closure and comfortably move on with ordinary business.

♦ *Use the sizzle to sell the steak* (**Sizzle Tactic**). The art of the sale is the ability of the salesperson to motivate the exchange of valuable items for those of less value, while maintaining the customer's belief that he got the better of the deal. In a casino, the gambler exchanges real money for the (supposedly real) opportunity to win a lot more money. But, the motivation for action, the sizzle of the steak, the thrill of the wager, exist only in the mind. To gain an advantage, to win a battle, it is necessary to provide your opponents with an appropriately motivating image, the sizzle factor. They must believe what you intend for them to believe so they will act in a predictable way.

The emotional content of your message (not the facts and figures) is the part of the message which convinces your customer to buy, or encourages your opponent to lay down his hand. If a person is emotionally involved in a product (that is, if she FEELS she will benefit from it), she will certainly buy it. Every person has a set of emotional triggers. When you are able to touch other people's emotional triggers, you have the keys to their motivation.

The senses (touch, sight, hearing, smell, taste) are gateways to the emotions. When we can sense something in our imagination, we begin to react emotionally to the stimulus. This is why the sizzle of the steak (nothing more than the sound produced when broiling a piece of meat), for a human carnivore at any rate, can produce an intense desire to acquire the steak and presumably consume it. Imagination is master key to manipulation. If you can reach into other people's imagination, you can produce whatever reaction you desire from them.

17

The SWORD in Hand

Tactics III

TACTICS BASED on Disguise require changing the appearance of actions so your opponent is not alerted to their true intent. Tactics using some type of disguise require boldness and daring because they may involve personal risk and close contact with (very often) intelligent and clever opponents. Success is directly related to your ability to create and maintain a false image.

On the other hand, when properly executed, tactics based on disguise are the most effective tactics available. Your opponents should have no idea that they are being deceived until the trap is sprung. When you are planning an operation based on disguise, think through your proposed actions methodically. Generally, you will be quite vulnerable while the plan unfolds. If something goes wrong, or you are betrayed, you will find yourself in a bad situation. Make sure you have a fire escape.

Tactics Based on Disguise

♦ *Knock on the front door, but enter through the back* (**False Focus Tactic**). Diverting your opponent's attention by some type of activity is probably the oldest tactic known. If your opponent is watching one area very closely, he may be ignoring another. Create a flurry of activity that will draw the focus of your opponent. While he is watching your obvious actions unfold, move your attacking force into position where he does not expect you. When you attack using the hidden force, the surprise and distraction should allow you to divide your competition and overwhelm his forces.

The False Focus Tactic is the heart of the four-step decision-action process discussed in Chapter 14, which we represent with the mnemonic S-K-W-R (Study the Flop; Know Starting Distributions; Wish and Want; Represent the Hand). Usually you will represent and bet your hand in a fairly straightforward manner. Occasionally, you will want to switch up on the other players by creating a false focus.

The easiest example of false focus occurs when you have flopped an extremely strong hand (say a full house). If you bet the hand out in a straightforward manner, you may end up making very little profit. If you create a false focus by betting the hand as if it were a straight draw, a flush draw, or even a weaker holding, another player may be able to catch up with a fairly good second-best hand, giving you some action you otherwise would not have gotten.

♦ *Routine actions degrade awareness* **(Familiarity Tactic).** Performing the same actions over and over again tends to reduce awareness in those people who are observing the actions. Familiarity fosters boredom. Boredom diminishes curiosity. New and unusual activity or strange behavior triggers alertness. But, if the same activity or behavior is repeated over and over again, it eventually becomes familiar and routine. If the routine is repeated for a long enough period of time, observers become desensitized to it.

For example, if you cannot hide activities that precede a certain tactical maneuver, start repeating those activities over and over again in plain sight for a period of time prior to the launching of your project. After a while, no one will even notice what you are up to. When the real deal starts, your opponents will be caught by surprise.

Many poker books mention the idea of "tells." As discussed in Chapter 6, a tell is an unconscious movement or sign given when a person is under stress. For instance, some people unconsciously twitch an eye when they are lying. Although a true tell is very hard to spot and to validate, inexperienced poker players are constantly looking for tells in others. Because of this, you may have the opportunity to provide false tells that will distract opponents who are looking for meaning in every little gesture you make.

One of the best false tells we have discovered involves the use of a card protector. A card protector is a small item, such as a coin or small stone, placed on top of your cards to protect them from being mucked accidently. If you acquire a card protector that has two sides to it, randomly switch the side that is facing up when you place it on your cards. We were doing this completely by accident at the table one night. To our surprise, we found out (from comments made) that other people actually observe whether the card protector is in its "heads" position or its "tails" position, and then try to figure out whether the position of the protector has predictive value for the pocket cards. This, of course, distracts them from concentrating on relevant factors.

♦ *Misinform through double agents* (**Spy Tactic**). Accurate and timely information is the key to developing and executing effective tactics. Whenever possible, provide misinformation to your opponent. When it is accepted and believed to be credible, misinformation is a powerful tool for creating an overwhelming advantage in interpersonal competition. The most effective method for disseminating misinformation is the double agent.

A *double agent* is an enemy spy who is working for you, either intentionally or unintentionally. Whenever enemy spies are discovered, their identity should be kept hidden and your knowledge of them kept secret. Once you know who is working for the enemy, you can insulate their access to information and utilize them by feeding them false data, which they will carry to the other side. The credibility of this kind of information is generally very high because the enemy will believe that it is coming from deep within your organization without your knowledge. Hence, your ability to deceive the enemy by using a double agent is greatly enhanced. Double agents are an invaluable asset.

Our modern world is full of spies, human and otherwise. To achieve success in the twenty-first century, you must be able to execute your plans, despite the fact that you are being passively or actively observed in nearly every facet of your life, at all times. On the other side of the issue, successful people must be able to obtain and utilize information to organize and facilitate planning and execution of tactics and projects.

Spying has ethical overtones. Looking into other peoples' lives without their knowledge or permission can be distasteful, or even illegal. Knowing that criminal, corporate, and government agents are looking into your life (right now!) without your permission is disquieting. But these aspects of our world will not be going away. The quality of your future and that of your children depends on your willingness and ability to profitably manage the conditions under which we all are compelled to function. Just like at the poker table, wishful thinking is the precursor of failure.

♦ *Signal right, but turn left* (**Feint Tactic**). Creating weakness in your opponent's defensive structure allows you to move strong forces against weak points. This is a key competitive principle. For an observant opponent who tends to act in response to your movements, a well-executed feint is designed to draw his forces toward the apparent target of your feint. To be successful, your feint must convince a skeptical and intelligent opponent that you actually intend to move toward the goal you are indicating. If your opponent does not believe your feint, your attacking forces may face a reinforced defensive position.

Successful feints are based upon effective use of faulty intelligence. Every bit of information that you are feeding the enemy must support the direction and nature of the maneuver you are making. If there are discrepancies in the messages you are sending, your competitor will become suspicious and may not take the bait when offered.

In poker, feints can be used to set up an opponent for a major takedown. For instance, you might want to bluff at the pot on a couple of occasions when you have no real reason to do so (and, of course, when it is relatively inexpensive). If you are called, make sure you show your cards in disgust to let people at the table know you are bluffing. In a later hand, when you have strength, play at the pot in the same fashion. If your feints have worked, other players may believe that you are trying another stupid bluff and call or raise you with weaker hands.

♦ *Borrow the hand that does the job* **(Hired Hand Tactic).** When you are involved in interpersonal competition, it is often inappropriate, or even dangerous, to directly confront a powerful or popular opponent. Under these circumstances, you must borrow the means to attack your opponent in order to keep your involvement under wraps and reduce your level of physical or reputational risk.

The use of a hired hand, however, introduces an additional element of risk to the situation. Anytime you are utilizing others to perform a difficult task, you are running the risk of failure on their part. There is no way to completely eliminate the risk of another's failure. Careful selection of the hired hands will reduce risk to some extent, but there is always the chance they will fail you, or turn up testifying against you at some future hearing.

We believe that many people will react to the previous paragraph with denial. After all, this is a book about poker, not an international spy thriller. If that is your reaction, think a moment. Have you not been involved in all sorts of plots and schemes in your life whose purpose was to affect, in some way, another person's life or business? Most of these (we hope, at least) were relatively harmless situations encountered in the normal transactions of life. But if something very important or very valuable were at stake, would you not utilize every means at your disposal to make sure you were successful? Of course you would.

The stated purpose of this book is to suggest ways to apply the logic of winning poker play to winning in interpersonal competition. No really good poker player would leave any possible avenue of advantage unexploited in his quest to win the game. He would go where he needed to go and use what he needed to use in order to win. If you intend to be the victor in the interpersonal contests you face, you should consider how you might do the same thing.

♦ *Donkey ears, shark eyes* **(Play Dumb Tactic).** The objective of the "play dumb tactic" is to induce your opponent to underestimate your abilities in a critical situation. An opponent who underestimates your abilities may be careless about preparing and executing actions when competing with you. A careless opponent is one of the greatest advantages you can have.

Playing dumb is a performing art. As is the case with any other performing art, the success or failure of a particular act depends upon the audience present. It is critical that you take a moment to judge the nature of the people you are performing in front of and how they evaluate the nature of "dumb play." The manner, method, and message of your act must be in concert with the expectations and capacity of your audience, or they will fail to appreciate, and consequently fail to reward your performance.

Good stories, good bluffs, good con games, and good acting all require suspension of disbelief combined with deferral of critical judgment on the part of the audience in order to succeed. People who are observing the performance must buy in to the premise of the story, bluff, con, or act before they can be moved to respond in the manner desired.

♦ *Bright smiles mask dark purposes* **(Iago Tactic).** A bright smile communicates warmth, friendship, and trust to others. A smile makes you attractive and approachable. It disarms the natural barriers between strangers. In short, it allows you to get close enough to your targets to do them harm. The less you suspect others of betrayal or aggression, the more dangerous they become to you. There is great potential for harm in allowing others to gain intimate access to your life. Trust provides an easy pathway for treachery.

The Iago tactic depends upon lowering other's defenses to the point where they no longer suspect you might be plotting against them. It is a strategy of deliberate betrayal of trust, and it works very well. Executing the Iago strategy involves personal risk. If your true intentions are exposed before you are able to act, you may face unpleasant or severe consequences. But if carefully developed, the Iago tactic can be carried out by one person acting alone. Acting alone limits the chances of premature disclosure of your intentions.

A smile, accompanied by a friendly attitude, certainly eases the tensions at the poker table. This can work for you in the sense that it reduces antagonism toward your successes. If you are a friendly winner, people may not resent it quite as much. Extreme clowning around arouses suspicions and antagonizes others. Overt attempts to be friendly can actually offend and annoy those players who prefer a cool and cautious atmosphere while playing. This may work to your advantage if you are able to put them on tilt.

◆ *Turn perception to reality* **(Golem Tactic).** As we have already noted, people's perceptions are filtered through models of reality based on background, education, culture, and personality. Decisions about the nature of reality based on these perceptions are controlled by the assumptions implicit within the models. People see what they believe; they do not believe what they see. You can use other peoples' beliefs and assumptions to create false reality.

The golem tactic involves creating a false or misleading reality based upon perception. The golem tactic is the essence of bluffing. In order for the golem tactic to succeed, you must understand the assumptions underlying another persons' view of reality. By manufacturing perceptions that interact properly with a person's set of assumptions, you can effectively create a reality for the person involved. The person will react to perceived reality in a predictable way.

Opportunistic bluffing is a necessary art in Texas Hold 'em. A bluff succeeds because the perceptions of the opposing player create a belief that he is holding the weaker or stronger hand. Hence, actions preceding the bluff must be consistent with those expected by the other player if you were actually holding the hand you are representing. Step four of our decision-action process recommends betting your hand from the beginning in such a way that your betting pattern supports the holding you want to represent. Most of the time you will be representing what you have. If done properly, other players will not be able to distinguish between situations where you are holding real hands and where you are betting represented hands.

The Thirty-Sixth Tactic

♦ *Combine and evolve* (**Spider's Web Tactic**). A spider cannot depend on a single strand of silk to capture his prey. Neither can you depend on one tactic to overcome your competition. Tactics need to be combined together and evolve naturally one into the next. In this way, you will weave a web of strategy from which your opponents cannot escape.

Appendix C contains a summary list of the Thirty-Six Stratagems as presented in Chapters 15 to 17.

PART FOUR

END GAME
AND RESULTS

Winning is the ultimate goal of playing a hand of Texas Hold 'em. Winning is also the ultimate goal of interpersonal competition. The specific definition of winning varies among people and situations, but some kind of *win* is absolutely necessary or you have wasted your time competing at all. Chapters 18 through 21 provide lessons in winning, getting your piece of the pot. Pay attention to factors in the end game in order to reap the results you want.

♠ ♣ ♡ ◇

18

Drowning
in the River

RETURN WITH us for a few moments to our imaginary poker
room, where you are comfortably involved in a $1/$3 No Limit
Texas Hold 'em ring game. Sitting at your table are a typical cast
of characters, including a ball-cap kid; several overweight, gray-
ing, nondescript men of indefinite age; an older oriental woman
(who, up to this point, is beating the daylights out of everyone
else at the table); and one younger woman, perfectly made-up,
with immaculately manicured nails (probably a dealer from
another casino).

Not wanting to waste the price of the book and allowing that we
may be at least partially correct in some of what we have written
here, you are following the better advice provided in the book (and
ignoring what you consider inappropriate). Hence, you are watching the other players carefully, you are opening pots, checking, calling, and/or raising with at least moderately strong hands. (Pocket
Scores of 35 and above, about 30 percent of your hands; see Chapter
12 for a review of the Pocket Score process.) For the hand under

observation, you are in the cutoff position, which is the position immediately to the right of the dealer button.

The dealer slides your cards across to you. The ball-cap kid under the gun raises to $12, the oriental woman calls, the younger woman calls. You look down at your cards and see A(h)K(d) [Pocket Score = 48], a fairly strong *drawing* hand in a relatively good position. You raise to $25; the button, small blind, and big blind fold; everyone else calls. Four players see the flop (ball-cap kid, oriental woman, younger woman, and you). You have position throughout the hand because you are acting last. There is $99 in the pot ($103 − $4 rake).

The flop comes A(d)K(c)4(d). According to P-I-C-K 'R, this is a paired, ranked, suited flop (no combo, certainly not rags). You have a very strong two pair, and the back-door diamond nut flush draw, but because the flop contains both A and K, plus two diamonds, it has almost surely hit one or more of the other three people in the hand.

You immediately decide that you will try to trap someone with your strong hand—or at least not drive anyone out of the hand right now—on the flop. Ball-cap kid checks; oriental woman bets $35 (one-third of the pot); younger woman folds; you call; ball-cap kid calls. Three players remain and the pot contains $99 + (3 × $35) = $204.

The turn card comes K(d), a wonderful card for you because it gives you a full house (Kings full of Aces), but it also completes a flush for someone holding two diamonds. You are really hoping someone else is holding two diamonds because they will certainly bet their flush, or at least call a bet. Ball-cap kid leads out with a bet of $100. Oriental woman considers the situation for several moments and then mucks her hand. You call. Two players remain and the pot contains $204 + $200 = $404.

The river comes 5(d), making four diamonds on the board, but because you have a completed full house (and also the nut flush), you are not worried about a stray diamond or two. Ball-cap kid rattles his chips around for awhile, restacking, and counting them. He has about $250 in front of him. After a moment's hesitation, he declares, "All in!"

All in? What the heck? There's no way your beautiful full house is beaten. You quickly call and happily expose your AK. Ball-cap kid nonchalantly turns over the 2(d) and 3(d) for a straight flush. A look of horror crosses your face. It's a straight flush all right, one of two possible hands that can beat your full house [the other being A(s)A(c), which results in Aces full of Kings, a better full house]. And, you have just flushed a few hundred dollars down the drain. A very tough beat. (For those of you who think this hand is improbable, you are right. But the events related above are based on a real hand played by real players in just this way.)

Considering the Alternatives

The objective of the story is to take a few minutes to consider whether you made any mistakes in the play of hand and how you could have played it differently. So let's analyze the hand and see what could have been done. We are not trying to point out any kind of specific mistake but rather the need to very carefully think through alternatives for each step in the progress of the hand. You can decide for yourself whether the analysis dictates the hand should have been played in a different manner.

The pocket cards dealt, A(h)K(d), represent a premium *drawing* hand. We make this emphasis because the large proportion of pocket card combinations are drawing hands. Pairs come along about once every 15 hands. The key to winning at poker is playing drawing hands well. Re-raising before the flop with a premium drawing hand like AK is probably a good idea. An AK(o) has about one-third chance to win the pot against three other players assuming they use reasonable starting hand distributions (25 percent to 35 percent of hands).

Why would your raise have been called by ball-cap kid with his holding of 2(d)3(d)? Initially, he put $12 in the pot under the gun (we assume the under-the-gun bet was a speculation on his part.) Your raise to $25 requires him to put an additional $13 in the pot. In a typical $1/$3 No Limit game, virtually no one who originally calls a bet pre-flop will fold to a small raise ($10 to $15).

Therefore, ball-cap kid would estimate he is getting $90 for his $13 bet ($103 total pot − $13 = $90), or almost 7 to 1 on his additional bet, assuming that the other players who called his initial bet will also call your raise. Even if ball-cap kid knew for sure you had AK(o), he would still have a 20 percent chance (4 to 1 underdog) of winning the hand with 2(d)3(d), providing him more than enough pot odds to continue, at least through the flop, so long as both other players also called. A raise to around $72 on your part would have reduced ball-cap kid's odds to less than the 4 to 1 he needed to call, even if the other two players were willing to call the raise.

The flop gives you two pair, Aces over Kings, which we noted above is a very strong holding, probably the current best hand. With a very strong hand, you can attempt to win the pot immediately by making a large enough bet to prevent players who are drawing to a straight or flush from getting the proper odds. Or, you can try to milk the hand for additional profit by making a bet that allows other players to call with straight or flush draws.

The flop [A(d)K(c)4(d)] gives ball-cap kid both a gut-shot straight draw, a flush draw, and a gut-shot straight flush draw with his holding of 2(d)3(d). He can count eight diamond outs for a flush [not including the 5(d) needed for the straight flush], two more non-diamond 5s for a straight, and the 5(d) for a straight flush, for a total of 11 outs. Oriental woman's bet of $35 puts $134 ($99 + $35) in the pot, giving him roughly 4 to 1 odds if you do not call, and 5 to 1 if you do. Because at 4 or 5 to 1, he has plenty of odds (after folding in some implied odds) to call $35, the question he needs to answer is this: Will he win the hand if he hits one of his outs? The best hand against him right now (on the flop) is three of a kind that his straight, flush, and straight flush beat, so he probably feels he could win with his outs.

You could obviously raise the flop here and discourage others from continuing. But with a chance to complete a full house by the river and a strong already made two pair, why would you want to prevent them from betting their almost certainly beaten hands? Therefore, you just call and wait to see the turn card.

The K(d) on the turn completes your full house (Kings full of Aces) and also completes ball-cap kid's rather weak diamond flush. He is first to act on the turn. He is facing a possible full house now that the board has paired. Why would he bet? If he doesn't bet, he feels one of his opponents will bet, since the K, which pairs the board even if it did not complete the full house, probably doesn't weaken anyone. If he checks, and someone else bets, he may need to fold; but he really wants to see the river card. Ball-cap kid's flush may also be the best hand, if other players are betting an Ace (and now hold two pair) or a King (and now hold three Kings).

So he bets $100 in the hope that everyone else folds, or that he will not be raised either because he really has the best hand, or the player with the better hand is hoping to get another bet out of him on the river. He also knows that if he hits his straight flush, he may collect all of the chips of the players remaining in the hand. He plans to fold if he is raised here, but you just call because you are indeed hoping to get another bet out of him on the river.

The river card comes 5(d). Ball-cap kid is again first to act. He takes his time putting in his bet in the hope you will become impatient and not think through what he might have. He is absolutely certain he has the best hand since a straight flush beats any hand possible given the board. He plays with his chips and makes all sorts of hesitant and unsure movements before going all-in. Ball-cap kid knows that the greatest fear a novice player has is the fear of being bluffed. His all-in move smacks of desperation and foolhardiness, a not-so-cleverly disguised and pathetic bluff on his part. If you do not take a few moments to consider that he might actually have a straight flush, you are going to bite on his bet without a qualm. Which you do.

Two Important Lessons

Back to the question at the heart of the discussion. Did you play the hand improperly? In real terms, probably not, since the chances of your being beaten were small once the turn card completed the full house. Could you have avoided losing the hand? Most likely yes, by raising enough on the flop or the turn to discourage anyone who was making a draw. Should you have raised? Arguable.

So the hand was just a bad beat and we can forget it, right? Wrong. There are two important lessons to be distilled from this hand. First, most of the time, people continue to play hands after they appear (at least to you) to be beaten because they have outs that will allow them to win the hand. Even, and in fact especially, when you have a powerhouse hand like a full house, you need to study the board for combinations that will defeat you. Anytime someone is betting into a board that makes his bet seem ridiculous, take a hard look for some combination of cards, however improbable, that might make the bet reasonable. If the combination exists, give at least a little thought to the possibility the person might have hit, or be drawing to, that combination of cards.

Second, when people make big bets on the river, they are generally not bluffing. Players who lob a sizable chunk of chips into the pot on the river usually have the nuts or close; we repeat, they are not bluffing. It is difficult to lay down a strong hand on the river and, therefore, very easy to convince yourself that your opponent could not possibly have outmaneuvered or outfoxed you. But the truth is that he has (on occasion). And you need to recognize it.

The economics of winning poker revolve around how capable you are of laying down losing hands. In the long run, everyone gets the same exact number of good hands; the difference between winning and losing money in poker is the ability to get away from losses. In every poker session, there are only a few hands that spell the difference between profit and loss. Most of the time, earning a profit is the result of not putting money in the pot after you are beaten.

Make a practice of hesitating a moment or two before committing to or calling a river bet. If you are even slightly unsure about your standing, minimize your losses. You will find that if you make a habit of attenuating your losses on the river, when you are unsure of your position, you will often avoid getting yourself into significant difficulty. We believe that if you were to make it a rule *never* to call an all-in bet on the river unless you have the absolute nuts, you would end up way ahead over your poker playing lifetime.

If there is one piece of advice in our book that you are willing to consider adding to your game, this is it. Throw away your hands, or at least minimize your bets, when someone else shows real strength on the river. Playing conservatively on the river will really save you a bunch of cash.

♤ ♧ ♡ ◇

<u>19</u>

Dimensions of Bluffing
I. Bluffing in Hold 'Em

THE WILLINGNESS and ability to execute an effective bluff is a fundamental skill for success in every area of interpersonal competition. In a general sense, a *bluff* is an indication (by word or act) of strength or weakness, conviction or doubt, intent or indecision, fact or fantasy that is designed to disguise reality and deceive another person. Bluffs are intentional misinformation; they are bold-faced lies. Bluffs employ leverage based on uncertainty and emotion.

The entire purpose of a bluff is to create a competitive advantage based on your opponent's misperception of reality—that is, to win because your opponents act based on a tainted or skewed impression of the facts of a situation. Often a good bluff allows you to win without fighting. As Sun Tzu puts it, "The greatest general is not the general who fights and wins one hundred battles, but the general who wins without fighting a battle at all." The best Hold 'em players are those who can win a large proportion of hands without having to show their cards. A good bluff can also allow you to win by causing your opponent to underestimate the strength of your position. Under these conditions, you expect a fight, but it will be one you can usually win.

In the narrow context of Texas Hold 'em, a *bluff* is any action designed to misinform other players about the value of the cards in your hand. A bluff is, therefore, a calculated bit of misinformation designed to steal or coerce the chips in the pot away from other players. The four-step decision-action process for betting hands, S-K-W-R, discussed in Chapter 14, anticipates that you will at least think about the possibility of running some kind of bluff whenever you analyze the flop.

Almost every Hold 'em hand played will involve a bluff or semi-bluff action (usually a bet, sometimes a tell) at some point. For example, a common bluff is an opening raise in the cutoff or hijack positions (one or two positions to the right of the button) in order to steal the blinds and antes. This kind of bluff is often executed with a very weak hand, and you can anticipate this move in a large proportion of situations where the pot is unopened until late position.

Because the opportunity to bluff is common in Hold 'em play and because players get a cheap thrill out of pulling off a bluff, even when the risks involved are greatly outweighed by the potential profits, bluffs are often attempted without much thought about whether the situation is really appropriate for a bluff or not. As we have pointed out previously, predictability in play is probably the greatest weakness found in Hold 'em players. If you tend to try the same tactic in the same situation on a regular basis, other players will be able to anticipate your action and use it against you.

Keep in mind that there are two types of bluff. The most commonly considered bluff is a bluff under conditions of weakness (*weak-hand bluff*). A weak-hand bluff attempts to convince an opponent that your position is stronger than it really is so he will retreat without a challenge. The other type of bluff is a bluff under conditions of strength (*strong-hand bluff*) where you attempt to convince your opponent that you are weaker than you really are so he challenges you when he should retreat and you are able to trap him. Both types of bluff are profitable when applied to appropriate situations.

Bluffing from Weakness

Let's take a quick look at the mathematics of bluffing from weakness. Bluffing from weakness can be quite profitable if you are able to reasonably estimate probabilities associated with your opponent's behavior. We believe that most players bluff from weakness far less often than they could. On the other hand, most players bluff from strength (try to trap) far more often than they should. Most players, even novices, are thoroughly familiar with executing a trapping strategy.

Assume there is $300 in the pot on the river; you have nothing more than a busted straight draw because the river card was a blank. There is a flush on the board and you are relatively sure your opponent has at least one pair, but not more than a straight (as a consequence, he is threatened by a potential flush; but if your opponent does call your river bet, you will lose). Your betting pattern through the turn is consistent with a flush draw. Your opponent checks to you. Under what conditions is a $100 bluff on the river profitable?

The analysis of profit goes like this: If the pot is $300, every time your opponent folds, you win $300 that you otherwise would have foregone. If your opponent calls or raises the bet, you lose $100 in addition to amounts already bet. Let's *assume* your opponents will fold 30 percent of the time to a $100 river bet. If we placed this bet ten times, we would win three times, out of ten tries, for a gross profit of $900 (3 × $300). We would lose seven times, out of ten tries, for a gross loss of $700 (7 × $100). Net profit for the ten bets is $900 (gross profit) − $700 (gross loss) = $200.

As a result, if an opponent will fold just 30 percent of the time, you make an average of $20 every time you bluff $100 on the river under these circumstances, even though seven out of ten times you lose the bet. The exact break-even point is a fold rate of 25 percent. (Wins in ten tries: 2.5 × $300 = $750; Losses: 7.5 × $100 = $750; Net Profit = $0.)

What about a $300 river bet (that is, a pot-sized bet in this case)? If your opponents fold 50 percent of the time, in ten tries you will win the pot five times for $1500 (5 × $300) gross profit; correspondingly, in ten tries, you will lose the bet five times for $1500 (5 × $300) gross loss, for a net profit of $0. Therefore, if opponents who would otherwise win the pot can be induced to fold 50 percent of the time or more, a pot-sized river bluff bet is profitable.

How do the mathematics of the bluff from weakness figure from the other side of the bluff (that is, you are the object of the bluff rather than the bluffer)? Look at a $100 river bet. If your opponent is bluffing 30 percent of the time, in ten tries when you call the bet, you will win $900 (3 × $300) and lose $700 (7 × $100), for a net profit of $200, or $20 every time you call. Further, the break-even point for the caller works out to 25 percent, the same as the break-even point for the bettor as calculated above. If your opponents are bluffing more than 25 percent of the time, calling a bet on the river is profitable for you.

It is our experience, however, as noted in Chapter 18, that players seldom (far less than 25 percent) make large weak-hand bluff bets on the river. Most of the time (because, again *we assume,* average players fear the significant cost of losing substantial weak-hand bets), a player will not be bluffing when placing a large river bet. As a consequence, we still believe you should avoid calling most larger river bets.

The issue in the mathematics of bluffing from weakness boils down to human behavior. Consider the issue carefully because in many instances successful weak-hand bluffing can spell the difference between a marginally profitable Hold 'em session and a solidly profitable one. We would speculate that response to bluffs, like most human behavior, is not linear. The likelihood of folding increases at an increasing rate as the size of the bet becomes larger (that is, in the shape of an upward sloping curve).

Therefore, it is far more likely an opponent would fold to a much larger (say, pot-sized) bet than to a smaller, more conservative bet. (This conclusion is, of course, common sense. But in support, one professional poker player we talked to suggested that the rate of opponents' folding in the face of well-conceived, pot-size river bets in cash games might be in the neighborhood of 80 percent. That's a substantially higher percentage than needed for larger weak-hand river bluff bets to be a hugely viable maneuver for him.) Hence, it might more profitable to consider placing larger bluff bets less frequently rather than placing smaller bluff bets more frequently. If your opponents *know that they* would not have placed so large a bet without a made hand, they will fold to your bluff every time. Knowing your enemy can make a huge difference in profit.

R-U-S-E

Bluffs, like other kinds of maneuvers, work best when used sparingly and selectively under conditions that are favorable to success. We use the keyword R-U-S-E to discuss aspects of an effective bluff during the play of a hand of Hold 'em.

....

The four concepts represented by the keyword R-U-S-E are:

Reality

Understanding

Set-up

Emotion

....

REALITY

The ability to see situations as they really are is the cornerstone of effective action; hence, *Reality* is the first concept in our keyword. We see reality through the lens of our mind's eye. To the extent that our mind's eye is adequately trained and focused, we will perceive reality adequately and consequently be able (more or less) to respond to circumstances in harmony with our goals and objectives.

Reality as it applies to executing a bluff has two aspects. First, you must perceive and evaluate reality consistent with conditions that exist. That is, you must assess the situation correctly. In a Texas Hold 'em hand, you must be able to evaluate your hand with respect to the other players' hands and appropriately estimate relative values.

Second, you must understand how to manipulate the perceptions of other players and be willing to accept the risks involved if you fail. In other words, you must read hands correctly and be willing to bet them in a way that effectively leads (or misleads) your opponents in the direction you desire.

The risks involved in bluffing a poker hand are either increased cost or decreased profit. In a bluff from weakness, you are attempting to convince your opponent you are stronger than you really are. The risk incurred is the possibility of losing the increased marginal bet you place as part of the attempt (thereby increasing cost). In a bluff from strength, you are attempting to convince your opponent you are weaker than you really are (usually by underbetting). The risk incurred is the possibility of losing the increased marginal benefit you might have received if you made a larger bet earlier (thereby decreasing profit).

UNDERSTANDING

Understanding relates to the ability of your opponent to correctly interpret your bet. The old saying is, "It is easier to bluff a good player than a bad player." Good players are able to recognize the implications of bets and will often respond to them appropriately (namely, by folding what appears to be a losing hand). Weaker, less experienced players, who do not understand the implications of certain bets, will not fold when they should, making weak-hand bluff bets less attractive. Before placing a large weak-hand bluff bet, make sure your opponent understands enough about the game to respond appropriately, at least some of the time.

Weaker, less experienced players are, on the other hand, easier to trap with a made hand, that is, with a strong-hand bluff. If you know your opponent is not that good at reading the potential combinations inherent in a board, you will be able to trap him more easily. If your opponent is also likely to call any bet holding only marginal hands (such as, top pair with a good kicker), you should aggressively attempt to trap him with your slightly stronger hands.

Trapping is especially possible with small pairs that turn into sets and second/third-high, two-pair hands when played against a board containing a lone Ace, King, or Queen. Inexperienced players typically overplay paired high cards with good kickers, and they can be trapped in their over-eagerness to win a pot by hands with combinations that are not obvious from reading the board (such as small two pair or small sets).

SET-UP

Every bluff must be *set-up* properly in order to succeed. The betting pattern of the hand and the make-up of the board must be consistent with the hand you are trying to represent. If there is inconsistency in the betting pattern or if the board composition is not really compatible with the hand you are representing, even weak players can become suspicious and react negatively. In fact, from the moment you sit down at a given table, every move you make must be considered a prelude to a future bluff. Your overall table image and play management, established over the course of many hands, will greatly influence how other players respond to moves you make in specific hand situations.

EMOTION

Emotion is the leverage behind a good bluff. People fear being bluffed. People become angry and flustered when they make a mistake. People are greedy for gain. People are overly vain when they make a successful play. (That is, most players mistake success grounded in purely good fortune with success grounded in skill.) Anytime you can interject emotion into another player's reasoning process, the subsequent decision has a chance of being faulty.

Any and every emotion will work if it serves to blunt another player's attention to the hand, even for a moment. Pay close attention to the foibles of other players. Use their emotions to leverage your play.

20

Dimensions of Bluffing
II. Bluffing in Interpersonal Competition

BLUFFING IN interpersonal competition has a significantly wider range of objectives and methods than bluffing in Texas Hold 'em. Interpersonal competition can be a complex jumble of means and methods, greed and grasping, ego and angst, courage and cowardice, self-preservation and self-persecution, sedition and sacrifice. Clearly, it really is a tangled web we weave when our objective is to deceive others.

Just as clearly, however, deception is a needed and necessary tool for success in almost all aspects of social life. The "General Theorem of Interpersonal Competition," which was presented in Chapter 1, is repeated here because of its importance:

Part 1
Every time you complete a move that convinces, compels, induces, or motivates another person to act in a way that benefits you, *when he would not have acted otherwise,* you gain.

Part 2
Every time you fail to complete a move that convinces, compels, induces, or motivates another person to act in a way that benefits you, *when the move could and should have been made,* you lose.

Part 3
Every time another person completes a move that is not to your benefit, *when you could and should have blocked the move,* you lose.

Part 4
Every time you are able to prevent another person from completing a move that is not to your benefit, *when you could and should have blocked the move,* you gain.

Implementing the "General Theorem of Interpersonal Competition" requires at least a minimal level of skill in deceiving other people. Further, because others are adept at deception and will use any chance you give them to gain something at your expense, detecting and deflecting deception is critical to your personal survival in business, career, wealth, power, and relationship issues. The greater your level of competence in deception, the greater your ability to run a successful bluff when necessary or when advantageous. The greater your awareness of methods used to deceive people, the more likely you will understand and counter deception when it is used against you.

The Elements of Deception
For purposes of discussion, we will partition the dimensions of bluffing and deception in interpersonal competition into four activities. To a large extent, the partitioning is arbitrary because these activities interact and overlap in real-life situations. We use the keyword S-E-A-L to organize the material about activities involved in interpersonal bluffing.

....

The activities represented by the keyword S-E-A-L are:
Seduction
Enlistment
Assurance
Lying

....

In turn, each activity has its own sub-keyword used to arrange ideas associated with using that particular activity to bluff and deceive.

Setting aside issues of ethics and morality for a moment (or, rather, placing those issues within the scope of individual conscience and choice), deception is another type of performance or act that must be practiced before the performance will be believable. Deception requires you to be completely aware of the image you project to others. Any adjustments to your image or your behavior that are intended to play a part in a bluff or deception project must be planned and practiced beforehand. Look for opportunities to rehearse your deceptive techniques when the stakes are low and results are not critical.

Bluffing and deception activities are a class of fiction created for specific competitive purposes. All fiction depends upon suspension of disbelief for effect. Each of the four activities considered in the keyword S-E-A-L relies upon some aspect of human character and/or social structure to anchor the activity and to provide a basis for creating a setting, an "ambience of legitimacy" if you will, that allows your target or mark (as in a con game) to suspend disbelief long enough for you to execute the deception. *Seduction* uses emotional bias as an anchor. *Enlistment* depends on social norms and beliefs. *Assurance* creates a contractual setting. *Lying* relies on alteration of facts.

A useful technique for gaining poise and confidence in performance of deceptive activities, particularly when practice subjects are not available, is *visualization*. Take a few moments each day to visualize yourself, in specific detail, successfully using one of the activities described in this chapter. Make a mental movie of yourself succeeding when you adopt a strategy based on some aspect of S-E-A-L. Visualization and physical rehearsal, if possible, will guarantee that you will have at least a feel for the activity involved before you need to perform for an audience.

S-E-A-L
SEDUCTION

Successful seduction is grounded in the unmet emotional needs of the marks or targets. If the marks' unmet emotional desires are strong enough, they can be deceived by seduction. Usually those needs are related to lust or greed, but other significant unfulfilled emotional desires can also be utilized.

....
The sub-keyword associated with seduction is W-A-N-T, which stands for:

Worth

Availability

Nuance

Touch
....

Worth: The first step in a seduction project is establishing *Worth* along one or more dimensions of the target's unmet emotional needs. If the target does not perceive and believe you can, in some fashion or other, fulfill her unmet needs, she will not be interested in you. You must, therefore, initially create the perception of worth in her mind.

Worth has an infinite number of aspects, all rooted in the value system of a unique individual. You cannot expect to know your target well enough at first to tap into her hidden value system. Fortunately, it is not necessary that the particular aspect of worth you establish initially be one that is directly related to deeper unmet needs. In the beginning, just be interesting to the individual you have targeted. Create an impression that you are someone who has some item or feature that makes you seem worthwhile to your target.

Availability: Once the impression of worth or desirability is created, the mark should be encouraged to believe that your particular worth is somehow limited in *availability*. Limited availability serves as a motivator and amplifier of interest for the target. Not only do you (as the seducer) have potential value, but you are in somewhat short supply. The elements of availability most often used are time and access. The target must be convinced that he can only gain the benefit of your desired feature if he is able to overcome the barrier or challenge of availability. Hence, he is encouraged to become deeply involved with striving to meet the requirements of availability that you have set.

Nuance: Nuance requires that you identify and address the mark's strongest unmet emotional need(s). Nuance carries the same goal as, say, customization for a new car. Every automobile carries within it the potential benefit of convenient transportation. The customer becomes excited and emotionally involved with the nuances, the specific parts of the machine that attract his individual proclivities and tastes. In order to impair your target's judgment sufficiently to run a bluff on him, you must "turn him on," in effect, with the details or nuances that he craves.

Touch: Emotional activity must reach a high enough level that it clouds or dispels the mark's ability to reason. She must desperately desire the nuances that you offer. Actual physical *touch* or strong mental pictures are required to link emotional need to nuance. In a sexual seduction, once the target has become engaged with the prize offered, emotional bonding can be accomplished by allowing the target to realize physical contact with the prize. As a substitute, clear and vivid descriptive or visual images can bind the target to the object of her desire, making it extremely difficult for her to disassociate the satisfaction of her unmet need with the object placed in front of her.

Seduction is designed to stroke the chords of emotion until the mark can only hear the tune you are playing. In today's world, we are constantly bombarded with attempts to seduce our judgment, so we have become somewhat immune to it. In order to work, seduction must be so carefully executed and so naturally performed that the target does not suspect she is being pursued. Seduction is potentially difficult and dangerous because its purpose is to arouse potent emotions. Practice it with an eye for your own safety.

ENLISTMENT

Enlistment is deception or bluff based on unmet social needs or unfulfilled social desires of the target. For example, people who have a desire to belong to a group—to receive group recognition, to feel safe in a group, to leech onto group status, to serve a group cause—can be recruited into the group and then used to further the group's objectives.

....

The sub-keyword for enlistment is I-M-A-G-E, which stands for:

Illustrate

Manipulate

Amplify

Gloss

Enfold

....

Illustrate: The first step in enlistment is to *illustrate* or advertise the existence and purpose of the group. Illustration should be directed toward individuals who have certain social needs or desires and designed to suggest that belonging to a particular group can somehow fulfill the desires of the individuals targeted. Providing examples of people who have already met their needs through group activities helps recruits understand how the group can fulfill their needs.

Manipulate: Enlistment is a highly personal process, much like a courtship. Once an individual has indicated an interest in the group, the mass market illustrations used to generate initial contact should be *manipulated* and fitted to an individual's specific needs. To accomplish this, potential recruits are turned over to specially trained group members (recruiters), whose mission is to manipulate the message of the group and the needs of the individual into a level of coherence that fosters a passion to join the group.

Amplify: The recruiter's job is to *amplify* the level of emotional commitment in the recruit. Amplification can take many forms, but its goal is always to replace rational judgment with emotional commitment. Note here, as in seduction above, that the greater the amplification of emotion in the subject of the enlistment, the more chance a lapse in judgment will occur.

Gloss: At some point in the process of recruitment, the potential new member will have some type of misgivings about his commitment to the group. It is critical for the group to be able to provide a *gloss,* or finish, to the enlistment process. The gloss is designed to hide any defects underneath a shiny surface until the recruit has passed the point of no return.

Enfold: Once the enlistment process is complete, the group will *enfold* the new members (usually with some kind of ritual) to reinforce their commitment and sense of belonging. The recruits pass from outsiders to insiders during the ritual. The group embraces them as full-fledged members with all rights, privileges, and duties of membership, and provides them with symbols of belonging. Symbols of membership are important and necessary to sustaining emotional commitment beyond the recruitment process. Symbols and rituals comprise the glue that sustains enthusiasm and maintains awareness of group cohesion over a longer period of time.

ASSURANCE

Deception by *assurance* relies upon the target's unmet need for the appearance of contractual or structural legitimacy. A surprisingly large number of people can be swayed by reference to apparently "legal" documents or other types of "official" statements signed and notarized by pseudo-experts or verified by external sources (like the Internet). Deception by assurance is used in almost every aspect of sales and marketing.

Two examples from our recent experiences will serve to illustrate how deception by assurance is commonly used:

1. We visited a car dealer to investigate trading in an older car for a newer vehicle. After quoting an unreasonably low value (what else?) for the older car, the salesman referred to an Internet site to verify the quote as being the "best he could do." He pointed to a computer, conveniently located nearby, and said if we could find a better price on the Internet, he would honor it. Of course, the site to which he referred us quoted very low prices for used cars. We went to an alternative site, which showed average market value for vehicles (much higher). The salesman was stuck because we had found another quote. Apparently no one prior to us had thought to use an alternative site to get around this particular assurance ploy.

2. While browsing through a sports memorabilia shop, we came across a somewhat out-of-place but nice Franklin Roosevelt autograph. We asked the dealer for proof of authenticity (a great concern for autograph collectors these days because counterfeiting signatures and documents is so easy). The dealer produced a signed and notarized statement from an "autograph expert," which said the expert had examined the piece and, from everything he could see, it was authentic. Judging from the dealer's surprised reaction when we questioned the authenticity of the expert also, most people must be willing to accept such assurance certificates at face value.

....

The sub-keyword for deception by assurance is S-I-G-N, which stands for:

Show

Involve

Graft

Notarize

....

Show: The objective of deception, in general, is to induce the target of the deception to suspend disbelief long enough to take the bait. In deception by assurance, the first step toward suspension of disbelief is to *show* the target the item or idea you are trying to sell him. Once you have put the item in the target's hands or have introduced the idea into his head, you should also show the target how he can satisfy his unmet emotional or physical needs by acquiring the item or idea you are peddling.

Involve: Bind the targets' interest by creating a bridge between their emotions and the service provided by your product. *Involve* their emotional satisfaction with the consequences of ownership of your goodies. People do not suspend their judgment because of logic or reason. They suspend their judgment because of emotion. Put them on some type of emotional tilt that can be satisfied only by you. At that point, you can maneuver them where you want them to go.

Graft: People who have need for assurance will eventually require you to produce enough proof of legitimacy or authenticity to satisfy their level of need. Your task is to *graft*, or splice, the proof you provide firmly into their decision process. Ideally, the grafting procedure will tightly meld whatever proof of legitimacy you have with their own preconceived models or standards. For example, if they tend to believe that computer printouts verify facts, then give them printouts. If they want a trusted celebrity to endorse the item you have, find an endorsee. Once your targets believe your proof is adequate, they will be willing to suspend their disbelief.

Notarize: Finally, deception by assurance requires some type of action that will *notarize*, or certify, the target's decision. That is, the client must make his mark, affix his signature, provide his stamp of approval. The physical action required to notarize his acceptance of the terms of the transaction completes the decision process for the client. The combination of emotional involvement with benefits derived from the product and physical activity seals the deal. Keep in mind, the heart of any effective deception consists of a mixture of emotional intensity (to destroy logical thinking and suspend disbelief) and physical action (to induce a commitment).

LYING

Lying is the act of deliberately misstating or distorting facts in order to induce others to reach conclusions that benefit the liar. Deception by lying is, and probably always will be, the most practiced and necessary form of deception. In Hold 'em, effective lying is the foundation of the art of bluffing. Success in interpersonal competition also requires a complete understanding of how to construct, deliver, and recognize a lie. Hence, we will focus our discussion on the four essential components of an effective lie.

....

The sub-keyword we employ is S-C-A-M, which stands for:

Simple

Credible

Accurate

Measured
....

The whole point of a lie is to communicate a distortion of fact. Communication occurs only when the sender of a message makes herself understood by the receiver of the message. The idea behind the keyword, S-C-A-M, is to emphasize the need to create understanding between sender and receiver. Whenever you decide to lie, make sure you achieve your objective.

Simple: Communication works best when ideas and method are *simple* and straightforward. Begin the process of communication by reducing the number and complexity of ideas to their most basic level. Your goal is understanding. Reducing the number and complexity of ideas presented will facilitate understanding by your audience. The wider the intellectual and social range of your audience, the simpler your message must be.

A good way to learn how to simplify your lies is to study political campaign slogans. An effective political slogan will say nothing substantive, but convey a broadly understood emotional impression. The objective is to make the electorate feel something for the candidate when it perceives the slogan. A perfect slogan would convey the exact emphasis required to attract voters across the broadest spectrum possible in the fewest words. "I Like Ike" said nothing substantive, nothing political, but conveys a tremendously positive message in simple, basic, and, importantly, emotional terms (unless you were backing Adlai Stevenson).

Credible: An effective lie must be *credible*. It may seem strange to talk about credibility with reference to creating a lie. A lie is a distortion of fact, but the fact being distorted is contained within a fabric of real events. The target of the lie does not know the truth (or the lie is worthless anyway), but is likely to have some partial knowledge of facts or events surrounding the situation. The fact being distorted, therefore, must fit within the fabric of known events. If your lie is to be believed by intelligent people, the lie must suit (at least superficially) the context of verifiable details.

Accurate: The details provided to substantiate the facts being distorted should be, to the largest extent possible, *accurate*. Nothing destroys a lie faster than small inaccuracies, or a story that changes slightly in the retelling. Know the facts of the circumstances and situation surrounding the fabrication. Keep them straight in your mind. Keep them simple. Reveal as little as possible, so your story can remain the same, even perhaps years after the original lie has been told.

If you have time to think through the lie, make an inventory of items related to the fabrication that must remain fixed in the telling so as not to alert an observant listener (or interrogator) to the possibility you may be making something up. This type of skilled performance requires practice. Use situations and chances where consequences are nominal to enhance your skills.

Measured: The word *measured* contains two related concepts. First, measured implies awareness of quantity or dose supplied. It is often necessary to consider how much fabrication is needed to reach your objective. If you create too much fiction, the sheer weight of the falsity will create suspicion. If you create too little, your message will contain holes in logic or substance that may reveal the true nature of the story. Just like Goldilocks, use neither too much nor too little, but just the right amount. Do not get carried away with your own cleverness.

Second, the word *measured* incorporates a sense of rhythm and timing. Rhythm and timing are required in any well-orchestrated performance. Without rhythm and timing, performances fall flat. As you are developing your strategy for deception by lying, consider the nature of the situation and the participants involved. How can you synchronize your message so it meshes smoothly with the other aspects of reality and falsehood that are intimately entwined in the circumstances? Your lie should be organized and delivered in such a way that it flows seamlessly into the stream of actual and synthetic events, matching the rhythm and timing of reality (as you wish it to be perceived) as neatly as possible. Careful consideration of rhythm and timing will yield results that are virtually indistinguishable from the real pieces of the puzzle.

The overall objective of a lie is to mask the truth in a way that benefits the liar. A mask is a device that alters the appearance of reality and communicates chosen characteristics to those watching. A good mask is like good make-up. Good make-up changes appearance in a desirable way without alerting an observer. Just so, an effective lie changes the appearance of the truth in a desired way without alerting a listener.

Lies, like masks or make-up, can be used, for example, to disguise, distort, (mis)direct, or deny reality. A lie used for disguise directly changes one fact into another without altering the greater part of the basic situation. It replaces the true fact with another fact of the same sort within the context of an event. A lie that distorts the truth indirectly changes reality by amplifying, exaggerating, diminishing, or minimizing certain features of the situation. A lie that employs misdirection focuses attention on certain aspects of a situation, while ignoring others. A lie that denies reality creates a substitute set of facts, which are mutually exclusive of the situation that actually occurred.

Match the content and structure of the lie to the type of mask you are required to create. But under all circumstances, keep your creation as objective and clearly stated as possible. Most lies are uncovered because the liar became too involved with his own fears. Think through the process and desired result carefully. Unless you want to fail, do not allow concerns of morality or correctness to unnecessarily complicate or cloud your thinking. Of course, it might be better—at least from the point of view of superficially acceptable interpersonal behavior—to consider not lying at all. Using the truth as your weapon in a bluff is always preferable, providing the truth is available on your side of the conflict.

♦　♦　♦

Bluffing in interpersonal competition requires understanding and appreciation of methods of deception. Situations in which important aspects of power and money are at stake will inevitably require you to be aware of the kinds of deception that might be used against you. On the other hand, sometimes it is impossible to avoid using deception to achieve your own goals. Taking the time to become proficient in deceiving others or defending oneself from deception when required (which is nearly always) can make the difference between accomplishment and failure.

21

Survival of
the Fittest

If you want a friend, get a dog.

—Old Bill from Ireland

There is no such thing as "Social Gambling." Either you are there to cut the other bloke's heart out and eat it, or you're a sucker. If you don't like this choice—don't gamble.

— Robert Heinlein, *The Notebooks of Lazarus Long*

You can always get bad advice from your friends, but [from] a good enemy, never! An intelligent, clever, resourceful adversary: now, he will teach you the real truth about yourself.

Sun Pin

When you walk through the doors of a card room, you enter into a place of convivial competition, animated interaction, and energized emotion. There you will find a spirited company populated by aristocrats, peasants, artisans, sportsmen, harlots, saints, investors, gamblers, sages, and fools. You can carelessly participate in a feisty game where wins can be, and are, loudly celebrated and losses can be, and are, silently regretted. Poker is a jolly pastime through which Dame Fortune cleverly substitutes good luck for real substance, real wisdom, and real courage; moreover, we poker players willingly, even joyfully, embrace her illusion.

Dare to step beyond the felted tables and clicking chips, however, and you will find yourself in a different kind of establishment—a smoky casino filled with self-delusion and fear—the place where the warp and woof of interpersonal competition weaves the fabric of ultimate success and failure. It is a dark, dirty, and dangerous venue filled with bad bets, surly dealers, harsh judgments, and even crueler consequences.

If you choose to enter that arena, you will confront chaos, challenge, and change. All you *think* you know may be turned inside out. The best you can hope for (but this is something to be cherished) is the chance to compete and to win at the highest level you can attain before someone or something takes you down. It is only there, in the pitiless playground of interpersonal competition, that you will discover and develop the fittest portion of yourself, that person within, who can survive and prosper on this marvelously entertaining plane of existence that we share with the rest of humanity, friends and foes alike. Of course the games are rigged, no doubt the stakes are too high, and naturally failure terrifies you. But the only way to win is to place your bets and reap the consequences.

The Five *Ills

As a way of summarizing and encapsulating the concepts contained in the previous twenty chapters (sort of compacting them into [P]ill form, if you will allow us to say it, so they are easy to swallow), we introduce the five *ills:

Will

Skill

Fill

Kill

BILL

Our use of assonant keywords to illustrate these five points is designed to help you remember and employ the concepts presented a long time after you have traded this particular volume off at the used book store.

WILL

Almost everyone we know has a wish to succeed, to accomplish goals and reach objectives that are somehow meaningful. The *will* to succeed, whether at Texas Hold 'em or interpersonal competition, requires a commitment to activity. Action is the trigger. What you do, you become. Talking about goals and objectives may create an appearance of ambition for a while, but action is the real thing.

Wherever you are and whatever your current financial, emotional, educational, or physical state, you can make a plan to move toward your goals. Pick the one thing you want the most in all the world and make a plan to acquire some small part of it. Execute the plan. Whether you succeed in the immediate action or not, you have begun the process of success. If you continue to act in the direction of your goals, you will eventually reach them, or whatever they have morphed into as a result of time and experience. All that is required is a strong enough will.

SKILL

There is a small persistent voice in the back of your mind that says that will is not enough; some things are simply beyond your capacity to accomplish because you do not know how. You must attain *skill*. High levels of accomplishment require high levels of knowledge. High levels of knowledge are obtained by first recognizing you need to learn (harnessing both arrogance and fear), finding out where to get the knowledge you need, and then applying your mind and your time to acquiring that knowledge.

Particularly with regard to a complicated technical subject like poker, it may appear that some excellent players have overnight success. Although it is true that certain individuals are more adept at learning the game than others, all champions, however young they seem, have traveled the path of practice and touched each and every base required. Knowledge combined with action opens the gates to whatever objectives you set. Find and acquire the skill you need.

The models we use to describe reality to ourselves shape the structure of the process we use to make decisions. Because the development of decision models is generally haphazard, they will create barriers to learning new skills and accepting new ideas. The keys to an open mind are humility and objectivity. The ego uses existing models to justify the reality we perceive. Humility and objectivity allow you to peel back the mental camouflage created by your background. Open your mind and open your world. Skill begins to develop when you decide that you, in fact, do not need to justify your lack of it.

FILL

The concept of probability surrounds and penetrates every second of our lives. Each and every moment of time is surrounded by an infinite number of possibilities, only a few of which will actually manifest themselves. In order to move toward our goals, we must make effective use of the cards we are dealt. We must employ the *fill* we actually get to create the reality we want.

The difference between frustration and satisfaction lies in shaping ourselves and our assumptions to fit the reality of circumstances. The bitterness we so commonly encounter in our fellow man is rooted in the false concept that things should happen in accordance with a set of preconceived and self-serving notions. We can only play the cards we are dealt. You must win your pots with these cards; you will receive no others, regardless of how deserving you are. Adapt your short-term goals to fit the situations you actually face, while keeping your longer-term objectives in mind. Remember that the opportunities you in fact get often lead to better outcomes than the opportunities you might wish for. Fulfillment comes from thoughtfully and creatively using the fill you get in the process of living.

KILL

All of the desire, all of the training, and all of the opportunity in the world cannot provide you with success unless you are willing to act when the time is right. The ability and willingness to *kill* means that you are prepared to do what is needed to accomplish and realize your plans. Sooner or later you will be required to risk your chips in a showdown. Either you will succeed or you won't. Picking the right showdown and executing effective measures at the appropriate time will certainly influence outcome. But in the last context, the fundamental absolute necessity for success is your determination to win. You must do what is necessary to get your work and your desires finished.

BILL

Cast your imagination into the future for a moment. You have will-ed, skill-ed, fill-ed, and kill-ed your way to the pinnacle of your personal and professional ambitions (whatever they may be). Now what? Did things turn out the way you wanted them to? Or are you overworked, stressed out, unloved, under attack, harassed, stalked, criticized, maligned, even shot at? Probably a lot more than you might want.

The one aspect of success that gets little play in the press is the aftermath. It is exciting to be involved in the uphill battle for prominence and prestige; the problem is the battle just gets worse when you reach the top because everyone wants to knock you off your perch or capture a piece of you. Here is one last keyword to ponder while you climb the ladder of achievement: B-I-L-L.

....
The actions represented by the keyword B-I-L-L stand for:
  Build a Base
  Interpret the Signs
  Locate the Exits
  Leave it Behind
....

♦ **Build a base.** Many people (including some fairly prominent poker players) are proud of the fact that they have made and lost several fortunes during their lives. Acquiring sufficient assets to be able to live in comfortable freedom is critically important, not only to you personally, but also to those who may look to you for sustenance and support. And making a fortune, even only one, is a real accomplishment. It should not be wasted, even only once.

When you begin to accumulate excess wealth as a result of your efforts, *build a base* that is strong enough to allow you to retreat when the time comes. No success lasts forever, nor does fortune bestow her favor continuously. Assume you will eventually fall upon harder times, so plan for them. If nothing else happens, you will get older. Don't waste everything you get.

♦ **Interpret the signs.** When you have begun to decline in effectiveness or influence, you will begin to experience that decline in the expressions and the actions of those around you, in the way people relate to you. Take the time to learn the signs of decline and *interpret the signs* effectively, especially with respect to yourself. When your time has come, acknowledge and accept it as inevitable. This will mark you as a superbly competent individual. Take your leave while you are on top. Creating success, and then getting out of it alive, is the ultimate achievement.

♦ **Locate the exits.** Whenever you enter a situation that has risk and challenge, be sure to *locate the exits.* Your opponents will not wait for a convenient moment (for you, that is) to plan and execute your retirement. Know your escape routes and slip through them quickly and quietly, if and when necessary. Trying to hang on to gains or glory when chance or circumstances have passed you by is the highest order of foolishness. Every exit leads toward the future, and there is always something new and interesting out there.

♦ **Leave it behind.** When it is over, leave it behind. In the last context, all you can retain is your opinion of yourself. With any luck, you will consider yourself to have done what you could with what you had to work with. The rest of the stuff is window dressing (although some of it is quite nice to have).

The only limits you have are those you put on yourself or those you allow others to establish for you.

Think about it. Now, check or bet!

APPENDIX A:
Texas Hold 'Em Fundamentals

A typical Texas Hold 'em poker game usually goes as follows:

1. Games start with the two players to the left of the dealer betting a predetermined amount of money so there is an initial deposit in the pot to get things started. The player with the plastic button in front of him is called the dealer; the actual dealer, a casino employee in a fancy shirt, does not participate in the game. This is called posting the blinds. There are two blinds, one big blind and one small blind. The big blind is usually one bet (i.e., in a $5/$10 game, it is $5). The small blind is one half a bet rounded down to the next lower whole dollar (i.e., in a $5/$10 game, it will usually be $2).

2. The actual dealer shuffles a complete deck of 52 playing cards.

3. Each player is dealt two cards face down. These are called your hole or pocket cards.

4. Before the flop is dealt (that is, before the first three common cards are dealt), there is a round of betting, starting with the player to the left of the two who posted the blinds (this player is referred to as "under the gun").

5. The amount a player can bet in the pre-flop round depends on what kind of game it is: Limit or No Limit. In a $5/$10 Limit game, the player under the gun can bet $5, raise to $10, or fold.

6. Like other games of poker, subsequent players during the first round can call, raise, or fold.

7. After the pre-flop betting round ends, the actual dealer discards the top card of the deck, called a burn card. This is done to prevent cheating.

8. The dealer then flips the next three cards face up on the table. These three cards are the flop. The flop cards are communal cards, which everyone can use in combination with their two pocket cards to form a five-card poker hand.

9. After the flop, there is another round of betting, starting with the first player still in the hand to the left of the dealer button.

10. After flop betting round concludes, the dealer burns another card and flips one more common card onto the center of the table. This card is called the turn card. Players can use the turn card, combined with any four other cards, to form a five-card poker hand. Sometimes the turn card helps; sometimes it hurts; sometimes it does nothing.

11. The first remaining player to the left of the dealer begins another round of betting (i.e., he can check or bet). In most games, this is where the bet size doubles. In a typical $5/$10 game, the minimum bet is now $10, with each raise being an additional $10.

12. After the turn round betting is finished, the dealer burns a card and places a final card face up in the center of the table. This card is called the river. Players can now use any combination of the five cards on the table and the two cards in their pocket to form a five-card poker hand.

13. There is one final round of betting, starting with the first remaining player to the left of the dealer.

14. After that, the players still in the game begin to reveal their hands. This begins with the player to the left of the last player to call. This segment of the game is called the showdown. If you are clearly beaten, you are not required to show your hand. You can throw it in face down. This is called mucking your hand. Be certain you have lost before mucking a hand. Once mucked in it cannot be retrieved.

15. The player who shows the best five-card poker hand wins! In cases where two or more players have equal hands, they divide the pot among them (this happens fairly often).

APPENDIX B: Pocket Scores

	Pocket Combo	Percent Wins Against 1 Random Hands	Percent Wins Against 2 Random Hands	Pocket Score	Number of Hands	
1	AA	85.3	73.4	70.0	6	
2	KK	82.4	68.9	66.0	6	
3	QQ	79.9	64.9	64.0	6	
4	JJ	77.5	61.2	62.0	6	
5	TT	75.1	57.7	60.0	6	
6	99	72.1	53.5	53.0	6	
7	88	69.1	49.9	51.0	6	
8	AKs	67.0	50.7	48.0	4	
9	77	66.2	46.4	49.0	6	
10	AQs	66.1	49.4	47.0	4	
11	AJs	65.4	48.2	46.0	4	
12	AKo	65.4	48.2	48.0	12	
13	ATs	64.7	47.1	45.0	4	
14	AQo	64.5	46.8	47.0	12	
15	AJo	63.6	45.6	46.0	12	
16	KQs	63.4	47.1	45.0	4	
17	KQo	61.4	44.4	45.0	12	
18	A9s	63.0	44.8	44.0	4	
19	ATo	62.9	44.4	45.0	12	
20	KJs	62.6	45.9	44.0	4	
21	KJo	60.6	43.1	44.0	12	

22	QJs	60.3	44.1	43.0	4	
23	A8s	62.1	43.7	43.0	4	
24	KTs	61.9	44.9	43.0	4	
				24.0	160	12.1%
18	KTo	59.9	42.0	43.0	12	
19	QJo	58.2	41.4	43.0	12	
17	A7s	61.1	42.6	42.0	4	
23	66	63.3	43.2	42.0	6	
24	K9s	60.0	42.4	42.0	4	
25	QTs	59.5	43.1	42.0	4	
26	QTo	57.4	40.2	42.0	12	
27	A6s	60.0	41.3	41.0	4	
28	K8s	58.5	40.2	41.0	4	
29	Q9s	57.9	40.7	41.0	4	
30	JTs	57.5	41.9	41.0	4	
31	JTo	55.4	39.0	41.0	12	
32	55	60.3	40.1	40.0	6	
33	A5s	59.9	41.4	40.0	4	
34	K7s	57.8	39.4	40.0	4	
35	Q8s	56.2	38.6	40.0	4	
36	J9s	55.8	39.6	40.0	4	
37	A9o	60.9	41.8	39.0	12	
				18.0	116	8.7%
38	A4s	58.9	40.4	39.0	4	
39	K6s	56.8	38.4	39.0	4	
40	Q7s	54.5	36.7	39.0	4	
41	T9s	54.3	38.9	39.0	4	
42	J8s	54.2	37.5	39.0	4	
43	A8o	60.1	40.8	38.0	12	
44	A3s	58.0	39.4	38.0	4	
45	44	57.0	36.8	38.0	6	

46	K5s	55.8	37.4	38.0	4	
47	Q6s	53.8	35.8	38.0	4	
48	T8s	52.6	36.9	38.0	4	
49	J7s	52.4	35.4	38.0	4	
50	A7o	59.1	39.4	37.0	12	
51	K9o	58.0	39.5	37.0	12	
52	A2s	57.0	38.5	37.0	4	
53	K4s	54.7	36.4	37.0	4	
54	Q5s	52.9	34.9	37.0	4	
55	98s	51.1	36.0	37.0	4	
56	T7s	51.0	34.9	37.0	4	
57	A6o	57.8	38.0	36.0	12	
58	K8o	56.3	37.2	36.0	12	
59	Q9o	55.5	37.6	36.0	12	
60	K3s	53.8	35.5	36.0	4	
61	97s	49.5	34.2	36.0	4	
62	A5o	57.7	38.2	35.0	12	
63	K7o	55.4	36.1	35.0	12	
64	Q8o	53.8	35.4	35.0	12	
65	J9o	53.4	36.5	35.0	12	
66	K2s	52.9	34.6	35.0	4	
67	87s	48.2	33.9	35.0	4	
68	76s	46.0	32.0	33.0	4	
69	65s	45.9	30.2	31.0	4	
				32.0	210	15.8%

APPENDIX C: The Thirty-Six Stratagems

TACTICS BASED ON STRENGTH

1. Beat the grass to startle the snakes (Snake in the Grass Tactic).

2. Use a loan to rob the bank (Other People's Money Tactic).

3. Remove the head and the body falls (Guillotine Tactic).

4. Fight a tired enemy (Play Hide and Seek Tactic).

5. If the head is protected, attack the feet (Achilles Heel Tactic).

6. Desperate people fight to the death (False Hope Tactic).

7. Confusion catches fish (Rattle the Cage Tactic).

TACTICS BASED ON WEAKNESS

8. Lure a tiger from his stronghold (Big Cat Tactic).

9. Keep strong friends over there and weak enemies close by (Weak Neighbor Tactic).

10. Arouse darker emotions to further your own schemes (Sin, Seduction, and Anger Tactic).

11. Arouse empathy with self-inflicted losses (Poor Puppy Tactic).

12. Hide weakness behind illogical actions (Stand Back Tactic).

13. Know when to run away (Hyena Tactic).

TACTICS BASED ON OPPORTUNITY

14. Steal a couple of sheep while the shepherd is busy elsewhere (Carpe Diem Tactic).

15. If you cannot attack your opponent directly, then steal his firewood (Short Supply Tactic).

16. Lock the doors while the thieves are still inside (Locked Door Tactic).

17. Watch a firefight from the other side of the river (Hands Off Tactic).

18. Lure your opponent onto the roof before removing his ladder (Up a Creek Tactic).

19. Loot a burning house (Hot Hand Tactic).

20. Replace solid beams with rotten timbers (House of Cards Tactic).

TACTICS BASED ON REPLACEMENT

21. Leave behind a golden shell (Shell Game Tactic).

22. Turn the guest into the host (Grab the Reins Tactic).

23. Aim right; shoot left (Innuendo Tactic).

24. Even false flowers look real from a distance (False Flower Tactic).

25. Breathe life into a corpse (CPR Tactic).

26. Keep a scapegoat handy (Scapegoat Tactic).

27. Use the sizzle to sell the steak (Sizzle Tactic).

TACTICS BASED ON DISGUISE

28. Knock on the front door, but enter through the back (False Focus Tactic).

29. Routine degrades awareness (Familiarity Tactic).

30. Misinform through double agents (Spy Tactic).

31. Signal right, but turn left (Feint Tactic).

32. Borrow the hand that does the job (Hired Hand Tactic).

33. Donkey ears; shark eyes (Play Dumb Tactic).

34. Bright smiles mask dark purposes (Iago Tactic).

35. Turn perception to reality (Golem Tactic).

THE THIRTY-SIXTH TACTIC

36. Combine and evolve (Spider's Web Tactic).

INDEX

Accurate lies, 203
Aces, 53
Achilles Heel tactic, 152–153
Advantage, creation of, 115
aggression, reasoned vs. over-the-top, 93
Alternatives, considering, 61–62
Amplifying, level of commitment, 199
Analyzing, answers to questions, 33
Angling for advantage, 50
Antagonizing, to encourage errors, 69
a-n-t-e (keyword), 81–83
Anticipating difficulty, 71
Anticipating risk, 82
Anxiety, as character flaw, 38, 40
Approach, as character trait, 43
arrogance, vs. audacity, 20–21
Asking the tough questions, 47–48
Assurance, in deception, 199–201
attitude, 8–9
audacity, vs. arrogance, 20–21
Availability, in seduction, 197

beats
    bad, 44

defined, 44
behavior
    dimensions, 90–91
    model, 90–91
    Oz-type matrix, 91–95
    quantum mechanics of, 88–89
Big Cat tactic, 154–155
"Big Slick," 145
b-i-l-l (keyword), 210–211
BILL tactics, 15
blinds
    defined, 20
    folding the, 20–21
bluff
    strong-hand, 187
    weak-hand, 187
bluffing, 14, 156–157
    defined, 186
    in interpersonal competition, 193–205
    opportunistic, 175–176
    purpose, 186
    set up in, 192
    in Texas Hold 'em, 186–192
    from weakness, 186–192
board, see flop board
Broadway, defined, 1–9
Building a base, 210

business situations
  competition in, *see* interpersonal
    competition
  decision making in, 3, 6–7
  decision risk analysis, 18
  expected value in, 24–25
  poker skills applied to, 25
  preconditions for, 18

career, *see* business situations
Carpe Diem tactic, 160
c-h-a-m-p (keyword), 42–44
chance, *see* probability
change, vs. stasis, 93
Chan, Johnny, 98
character, 8–9
character flaws, 38–41
  management of, 76
  mitigation of, 42–44
Compensation, as transferable
    benefit, 115–116
confidence, 76
  need for, 37
  and power to act, 76
Conform, Collect, Construct
    action, 79–80
counting outs, 131–134
Courage, as character trait, 42
CPR tactic, 166
Credible lies, 203
Crowding, to encourage errors,
    69
Curiosity, arousing, 102

deception, elements of, 194–196
decision making
  effective process, 32
  models for, 113
  single static measure for, 135
decision model, for business situa-
    tions, 6–7
Defending, 68
Desire, Decide, Detail action,
    77–78

Developing constancy, 49
d-i-c-e (keyword), 77–81
Dion, Celine, 43
d-i-s-c-a-r-d (keyword), 67–70
Distracting, to encourage errors,
    70
Drawing hands, 54

Effectuating action, 79–80
Ego bets, 54–55
Eisenhower, Dwight, 59
emotion
  in bluffing, 192
  vs. common sense, 19
  gaining control over, 22, 24
emotional intensity, 79
Empathy, establishing, 102
End game, 14
Enfolding, of new members, 199
Enlistment, in deception,
    198–199
Entering the arena, 73
errors
  changing starting-hand selection,
    17–18
  encouraging in others, 67–70
  vs. failure, 65–66
  mismanaging the stake, 20
  misreading the situation, 18–19
  protecting against, 70–74
Evolution
  of ideas, 116
  of situation, 60
Exiting on cue, 74
Expecting deceit, 83
Experimenting to evolve, 34–35

facts, vs. opinions, 92–93
failure
  avoidance of, 76
  causes of, 65–66
  defined, 65
  vs. errors, 65–66
  tolerance of, 35–36

False Flower tactic, 165–166
False Focus tactic, 169–170
False Hope tactic, 153
Familiarity tactic, 170–171
Feint tactic, 172–173
Ferguson, Chris, 93
Fill tactics, 15, 209
flop
    computing pot odds, 134–136
    counting "outs," 131–134
    defined, 120
    as force of change, 10–11
    playing decisions, 137–147
    reading pocket cards, 119–127
    reading the board, 128–131
flop board
    combo board, 130
    paired board, 129
    rags board, 131
    ranked board, 131
    suited board, 129–30
flush draw, defined, 129
Friedman, Prahlad, 40
"Fundamental Theorem of Poker"
    (Sklansky), 4

"General Theorem of Interpersonal
    Competition," 4–5, 193–194
Gloss, in deception, 199
Gold, Jamie, 94
Golem tactic, 175
Grabbing the Reins tactic,
    164–165
Grafting the proof, 201
Guillotine tactic, 152

Hachem, Joe, 94
Handling the cards, 47
Hansen, Gus, 51, 98
h-a-r-d w-a-y (keyword), 46–51
heads-up competition, 53
Heinlein, Robert, 12, 206
Helmuth, Phil, 94, 97
Hickok, Wild Bill, 1

Hired Hand tactic, 173–174
Holden, Anthony, 1
Holding up your end, 72
Hot Hand tactic, 162
House of Cards tactic, 163
human behavior, *see* behavior
Humility, as character trait, 43
Hyena tactic, 157

Iago tactic, 174–175
i-c-e (keyword), 102
ideas, *vs.* rules, 93
illusion, *vs.* substance, 93
Illustrating, 198
i-m-a-g-e (keyword), 198–199
Imagination, stimulating, 102
Imitating the best, 73
Inflating, to encourage errors,
    68–69
Innuendo tactic, 165
Inquiring, 101–102
inside straight draw, defined,
    132
interpersonal competition
    bluffing in, 193–205
    decision making as key in, 3
    examining prospects prior to,
        60–63
    five truths of, 11–12
    fundamental theory of, 4–5
Interpreting the signs, 211
Invest, Intensify action, 78–79
Involving the target, 201
Ivey, Phil, 98

Kill tactics, 15, 209–210
Kinetics, dynamics of the flop,
    10–11
Kneeling to power, 72
Knowing starting distributions,
    138

Land of Oz
    behavioral nodes, 92–93

Land of Oz (continued)
  characters, 93–95
  matrix, 91
  typecasting with sonar, 100–105
laying down hands, discipline for,
  55
Leaving it behind, 211
Lies
  to deceive, 202–205
  measured, 203–204
  objective of, 204
  single, 202
Limit Hold 'em, vs. No Limit Hold
  'em, 31
Lion (bureaucrat), 93–94, 105
Lisandro, Jeff, 40
Living like someone is watching,
  73
Locating the exits, 211
Locked Door tactic, 161–162
logic
  application of, 76
  effective use of, 56–57, 64
Loving your neighbor, 71–72
Low Limit Hold 'em games, pre-
  flop betting in, 111
luck
  effect on outcomes, 76
  role of, 45–46
  rules for staying out of trouble,
    51–54

Manipulating, 198–199
m-a-p (keyword), 17
m-a-s-t (keyword), 32–33, 34, 91
Matusow, Mike, 94
Means and methods, as character
  trait, 43
Measured lies, 203–204
Measuring, 32–33
m-e-l-t (keyword), 103, 104–105

negotiation, initial rounds
  strategies, 11

Negreanu, Daniel, 51, 94, 107
No Limit Hold 'em
  vs. Limit Hold 'em, 31
  pre-flop betting in, 112
  size of pots, 69
Nose to the ground, 73
Notarizing the decision, 201
n-o-t-e (keyword), 57–60
Nuance, in seduction, 197
Numbers rule, understanding the
  math, 82–83
nut flush, 54
nut straight, 54

opening-hand selection
  as key decision, 106
  25-percent range, 107
  POCKET Score for, 108–109
opportunity seeking, vs. avoiding
  mistakes, 93
Organizing facts, 31–32
orphan flops, 146–147
Other People's Money tactic, 152
outcome, reaching desirable,
  43–44
outcomes
  being aware of, 59
  decision model for predicting,
    113–114
outs, defined, 34
overcard, defined, 53
Oz, see Land of Oz

Pairs, 52–53
  types of, 52–53
patience, need for, 21–23
People, interrelationship of, 115
p-i-c-k 'r (keyword), 128–131
p-i-n-g (keyword), 100–105
Play Dumb tactic, 174
Play Hide and Seek tactic, 152
playing the player, 87–88
POCKET Scores
  sample computation, 109

sample score, 108–109
summary table, 216–218
Point of attack, choosing the,
62–63
poker, see also Texas Hold 'em
fundamental theory of, 4
as keyword, 1–14
as theme in movies and TV
shows, 1–2
Poor Puppy tactic, 156
Posing, 100–101
Position, character and attitude, 8
pot, expected value of, 134
pot odds, computing, 134–136
power, see business situations
p-o-w-e-r (keyword), 30–36
pre-flop betting, 111–13
patterns, 120–121
pre-flop positions
dealer position, 110
evaluating, 110–111
under-the-gun position, 110
Preparing to choose, 30–31
levels of choice, 31
probability
calculation of, 23
expected value, 24
vs. skill, 21

rainbow flop, 131
ranked card, defined, 127
r-a-p-t (keyword), 61–63
r-a-t-s-s (keyword), 39–41
Rattle the Cage tactic, 153
Readiness, determining level of, 61
Reality, in bluffing, 190–191
Recklessness, as character flaw, 38,
40
Reducing the field
to improve the odds, 47–48
as intimidation tactic, 69
using smear campaigns, 48
relationships, see business situations

Representing the hand, 139
requirements, 75–81
Results, 13–14
rewarding yourself for remembering, 35–36
risk and reward, evaluation of,
81–83
rules, vs. ideas, 93
r-u-s-e (keyword), 190–192

s-c-a-m (keyword), 202–204
Scapegoat tactic, 166–167
Scarecrow (analyst), 93, 105
Scaring, as intimidation tactic, 69
s-e-a-l (keyword), 14, 195–197
Seduction, 196–198
seeking gain, vs. avoiding
loss, 93
Self-importance, as character flaw,
38, 41
set, defined, 44
Set-up, in bluffing, 192
Shell Game tactic, 164
George Washington example,
164
Short Supply tactic, 160–161
Short-temperedness, as character
flaw, 38, 41
Showing the item or idea,
200–201
s-i-g-n (keyword), 200–201
Simple lies, 202
Sin, Seduction, and Anger tactic,
155–156
situation, being aware of the, 58
Sizzle tactic, 167–168
Skill tactics, 15, 208–209
Sklansky, David, 4, 5
s-k-w-r (keyword), 137–139, 170
slow play, defined, 121
Snake in the Grass tactic,
151–152
s-p-a-c-e (keyword), 114–116
s-p-a-d-e (keyword), 51–54

Specifications, for creating change, 115

Spider's Web tactic, 176

Spy tactic, 171–172

stake, management of, 20

Stand Back tactic, 156–157

starting hands, 51–52
  analysis of, 122–125
  15-percent distribution, 123
  implications of, 125–126
  playable combinations, 17–18
  playing AK offsuited, 145–146
  playing KQ offsuited, 142
  playing paired jacks, 140–141
  playing 78 suited, 143–144
  selection of, 17–18
  for subsequent players, 126–127
  30-percent distribution, 124–126
  20-percent distribution, 123–124

straight draw, defined, 130

Studying the flop, 138

substance, vs. illusion, 93

Sun Pin, 206

Sun Tzu
  on attacking weakness with
    strength, 62
  on causes of failure, 66
  on character flaws, 38–39
  on deceiving the enemy, 117
  on expecting the worst, 59
  on knowing your enemy, 57, 99
  on opportunity, 85
  on tactics and strategy, 11
  on winning without fighting,
    187

s-w-o-r-d (keyword), 13, 119
  tactics, 150

Synthesizing, 33

tactics, 59–60, *see also Thirty-Six
    Stratagems, The*
  developing winning, 59–60
  objectivity and humility, 12
  vs. strategies, 11

t-a-l-k (keyword), 103–104

Targeting gains and losses, 83

tells
  Aggression, 103
  body language, 104
  defined, 63
  Eye movements, 104
  Key/Tone of voice, 104
  Language, 103–104
  Lips tightening, 105
  Tension, 103
  Trembling, 105

Testing, 33

Texas Hold 'em
  behavioral patterns in, 89–95
  bluffing in, 186–192
  expected value in, 24–25
  five *ills, 15
  as foundation for business
    tactics, 2
  fundamentals, 213–215
  as game of skill, 22
  mistakes made in, 17–18
  as model for interpersonal
    decisions, 2–3, 5
  pre-flop strategy, 9–10
  sample scenario, 179–183
  tolerance for failure in, 35–36
  using logic in, 56–57, 64

Thinking success, 72

Thirty-Six Stratagems, The, 13,
    149–150
  tactics based on disguise,
    169–176, 220–221
  tactics based on opportunity,
    160–163, 220
  tactics based on replacement,
    163–168, 220
  tactics based on strength,
    151–154, 219
  tactics based on weakness,
    154–158, 219
  thirty-sixth tactic, 176, 221

Timidity, 38, 41

as character flaw, 38, 41
Timing, as key to success, 63
Tin Man (executive), 94, 105
Touch, in seduction, 197
trapping, 191
trips, defined, 44

Understanding, in bluffing, 191
Up a Creek tactic, 162

visualization, 195

Waiting and watching, 49–50
copying the lions, 49–50

w-a-l-k t-h-e l-i-n-e (keyword),
71–74
w-a-n-t (keyword), 196–197
Watching your step, 71
Weak Neighbor tactic, 155
weakness, management of, 66–67
wealth, *see* business situations
Welding to wield, 33–34
Will tactics, 15, 208
Wishing and wanting, 138–139
Wizard (politician), 94, 105
Worth, in seduction, 196

Yes! Saying "yes," 50